What People Are Sa

"Not That God reminds us that what we think about when we think about God is of utmost importance. Ryan Smith skillfully unpacks the story of Lazarus from John 11, and in doing so challenges us to reframe our fears and doubts in the context of a sovereign God. If you struggle with believing that God's answers and timing are always right, this book will be of great service to you. Pastoral without being preachy, Ryan helps the reader understand that in order to get the right answers, we must start with the right questions."

Danny Franks - Connections Pastor, The Summit Church - Durham, North Carolina.

"Ryan Smith loves the Lord and His church. He brings a wonderful creativity combined with a grounded theology to every issue. He connects with real people and the everyday ministry of the local church; thus, what he has to say rings with authenticity. I thank the Lord for Ryan, his ministry and this contribution."

Dr. Hance Dilbeck - Senior Pastor, Quail Springs Baptist Church - Oklahoma City, Oklahoma

"If you have questions and doubts, if you've found yourself feeling like you are waiting on God or disappointed with Him, this book is for you. Ryan does a wonderful job of identifying and wrestling with some of the tensions and challenges we face as we seek to trust in God. The book is honest, insightful, stirring, challenging and truly helpful."

Curtis Cook – Pastor, Hope Fellowship Church - Cambridge, Massachusetts.

"Before chapter one was over, I found myself on the edge of my seat crying out, 'Who is this Jesus who spawned controversy, conflict and crises? If He brings all of this, is he still the same Jesus who claims to be the essence of all hope, goodness, joy and salvation? Can I trust this Jesus? Is this the Jesus I know and proclaim? Who is this God who can flip over the tables of my life and yet calm the storms of my soul?' Ryan poetically intertwines story, experience, and theology to identify the God of John 11 who can do all this and more."

KC Maddox – Pastor, Free City Church - Lawrence, Kansas

NOT THAT GOD

Trading the Believable Lie for the Unbelievable Truth

RYAN ANDREW SMITH

WESTBOW
PRESS®
A DIVISION OF THOMAS NELSON
& ZONDERVAN

Scripture quotations are from The Holy Bible, English Standard
Version® (ESV®), copyright © 2001 by Crossway, a publishing ministry
of Good News Publishers. Used by permission. All rights reserved.

WestBow Press books may be ordered through booksellers or by contacting:

WestBow Press
A Division of Thomas Nelson & Zondervan
1663 Liberty Drive
Bloomington, IN 47403
www.westbowpress.com
1 (866) 928-1240

Author photo by Karen Lemley

ISBN: 978-1-5127-0667-3 (sc)
ISBN: 978-1-5127-0668-0 (hc)
ISBN: 978-1-5127-0666-6 (e)

Library of Congress Control Number: 2015912661

Print information available on the last page.

WestBow Press rev. date: 08/07/2015

Contents

To Allison and Kelen,
you are such amazing signs of God's grace to me.

And to my family.

For the Lord is good;
his steadfast love endures forever
and his faithfulness to all generations.
—Psalm 100:5

Acknowledgments

No book is written alone. Special thanks goes to John Piper, John MacArthur, Frederick Dale Bruner, Merrill C. Tenney, John Calvin, R. C. Sproul, and R. Kent Hughes for your written resources and insights regarding the book of John.

Thank you to Blue Spruce (Stillwater, Oklahoma), Aspen Coffee (Stillwater, Oklahoma), Wesley Owens Coffee (Monument, Colorado), Lost Coffee (Castle Rock, Colorado), and a few others for your inviting atmosphere and caffeinated encouragement throughout the writing process.

Thank you, Cole Feix, for your friendship, partnership in the gospel, and insights as we worked through these ideas (especially your contribution to chapter 3).

Thank you, Brent Prentice, for serving as an excellent and humble leader in Christ. Our dialogue and partnership has been integral in the creation of this project.

Special thanks to my lovely wife, Allison, our son, Kelen, and my parents, Dan and Julia Smith, for your encouragement and sacrificial support.

Thank you to our Eagle Heights church family (eagleheights. com) for giving me the time and energy to invest in this project. It is a joy to be in community with you.

Most of all I thank God—Father, Son, and Spirit. May this serve for your glory alone.

Introduction

He had been coming to our group for a few weeks. His hesitation was apparent. He was different from most of the group, but I don't think he completely knew it. He set himself apart by his tattoos, pierced lip, and punk-rock veneer, but it was easy to see those were simply "no trespassing" signs. As the warm welcome slowly melted away his layers of insecurity, there was a sense that he was beginning to feel at home. I wanted him to feel at home.

He had been hurt. This wasn't something he said outright. In fact, he said very few things at all. But you could tell. He wanted to be loved. He wanted answers to so many questions. He wanted to know God, but he wasn't sure about the God he did or did not believe in.

We'll call him Mark. After a few weeks of distance, Mark had come to be at home with us. I hoped he would stay.

As the five-minute countdown was displayed on the screen and the group slowly filtered toward the seats, I saw Mark run in the back door. He was upset. He was lost, and he came running to one of the few homes he had known.

In my mind I was rehearsing the message. I was thinking logistics. As he ran up to me, the countdown continued to march forward. The pressure of time was on me. A greater pressure was crushing Mark.

We stepped to the side, and he wept. I put my arm around him. My prayers immediately flowed for him, yet one eye was still on the descending numbers on the screen.

As Mark began to compose himself, I asked him what was wrong. Through gulping sobs, he told me he had just learned his father was sick—very sick. While his father was remaining strong and attempting to cast a good light on the situation, Mark knew what was coming.

He couldn't tell me much, but he didn't need to. Mark was confused. How could this be happening? He was only seventeen. Seventeen-year-olds need their dads. They are supposed to have their dads. God is supposed to give them their dads. Whatever foundation of belief he had been laying about God was caught in a windstorm of doubt, fear, and insecurity.

I didn't know what to say. Nothing prepares you for this. I asked what his dad's name was and began to pray for him. It wasn't what Mark wanted, but he resigned himself to it. As the countdown reached a minute and thirty seconds, I asked him to stay for the group time. I planned to talk with Mark about what he was going through after the gathering. Mark didn't want to talk (1:00). It became clear he wasn't so much asking me for something as he was telling me.

Time was running short. I knew I had to make a decision. Mark made it for me. Everything he had been learning (45 seconds), everything he had heard about the goodness and love of God was in the throes of a raging tempest (30 seconds). He had been hurt before (15 seconds). He was hurt again (10 seconds). All I could say was, "I'm so sorry." He turned and ran down the hall (5 seconds). I turned and looked at the clock (3 seconds, 2 seconds, 1 second). It was time to go talk about the goodness of God.

A. W. Tozer said, "What comes into our minds when we think about God is the most important thing about us."[1] It saturates who we are. Our theistic worldview drips everywhere we go. Nothing affects our inner and outer lives—how we pray, how we walk through joy and suffering—more than this.

Our view of God and the world is largely informed by how we define certain words like *good*, *bad*, *fair*, and *love*. This is significant for us because we use these words to define our perceived past, present, and future. We are taught the meanings of these words from a very young age. My three-year-old knows these words and uses them loosely. However, as we walk through life and interact with others, we are continually molding redefinitions and reapplications of these terms.

Our definitions of these words greatly influence what becomes our worldview. Our worldview is a sort of lens through which we perceive the world. Everyone's lens is different. It doesn't make the world different. It simply shapes how we uniquely understand it. Our worldview may be shaded or smeared by certain experiences, hurts, or areas of perceived conflict avoidance.

There is a question I want to ask throughout this book: *What if our worldview is different than God's?* In other words, what if *our* definitions of these terms inform our view of God, ourselves, and our circumstances more than God's definitions? That is an important question. It causes tension and leads to investigation. The vast majority of this book is written so that people can read from that place—in the land of investigative tension. This is a good place to be. God continually places us here to produce faith or reveal our true hearts. It is a refining fire.

This is a good place, but I know it is a difficult one. I don't know why you are reading this book. You may not either. Perhaps someone gave it to you or recommended it. Maybe your own curiosity about God and life has led you to this resource. No matter who you are or why you are reading this book, I do know something about you. You are going through a difficulty, have gone through difficulty, will go through difficulty, or want to walk alongside someone else in one of these categories.

I've titled this book *Not That God*. As we walk through these challenging issues and ideas, I want us to be informed by something greater than our preconceived notions or perspectives about God. I want us to walk through the Bible. It is the sufficient, inerrant, authoritative resource God has given us to filter and understand reality.

Specifically we are going to journey through John 11:1 to 12:13. The reason I've chosen this passage is because Jesus does several things that make me uncomfortable in it. The story doesn't go how I would have written it. Perhaps there are parts I can immediately get on board with, but other parts cause me to question or hesitate about the God I have believed in. Here John pushes on my preconceived notions of Jesus, and it is a sensitive spot.

In John 11, Jesus reveals himself to be a different God than people had hoped for. He is a Jesus who values his glory above our comfort, the eternal over temporal, and his ways above ours. In every way this is difficult yet best for us. This presents a tension we will embrace, ignore, or snap from. This is important.

Because it is so important, we need to test our faith. We need to test the spirits and ask an important question. *Could we be acting toward and reacting to a God contrary to the one revealed in Scripture, one of our own cultural making or desire, a god who lives simply to make us comfortable?*

What if the true God of the Bible is the God we don't believe in? What if the God of the Bible is much better?

We live in a world where pain and questions exist. The Bible clearly shows us these are not reasons to doubt God. Rather they are intended to inform how we know and relate to God and the gospel. However, this is not an easy process.

Pain is never easy. Difficulty is seldom expected and rarely seen as a cause for joy and growth. You may have experienced a lot of loss in a short period of time. Maybe you feel your life is continually marked by loss, waiting, and doubt. Some of you have received difficult answers. Some of you are waiting on answers to difficult questions.

Our short passage captures one of Jesus's greatest miracles. It also raises a lot of questions and opposition. It is a story in which Jesus raises a man from the dead. But he also lets someone die. He lets a community grieve.

I want this book and this passage of Scripture to push and prod us. However, I know it will push and prod where some of us are very sore. My heart is heavy because for some of us, these discussions will hit very close to home. I am also glad because that is what the Bible should do. It is how we grow. It is how reality is revealed to us, and strength is gained as our spiritual muscles ache.

This book and these topics are offered not to hurt but to heal, not to bind but to loosen, not to break down but to build up. I want you to be equipped. If there is anything I can give you to put in your spiritual backpack as we journey toward what is to come, I want you to know who Jesus actually is and have life in his name.

As you read these chapters, please do not hear me simply saying, "Get over it," or, "That's the way it is, so get on board or get left behind," in response to your trials. If people had said that to me (or used the Bible to say that to me) in certain periods of my life, I probably would have punched them in the mouth ... with gusto.

Whether you are in a season of joy or pain, filled with peace and confidence, or in doubt and despair, I want to talk with you right where you are. In each of these seasons—and we will go through all of them—I want us to have a right view of God. So wherever you are, no matter where you are headed, and no matter where you have been, you are in the right place to read this book.

Read with an open heart and mind. Start from this place: *God is the end, not the means.* Don't read this to see how you can use God to get something else. You can lose weight, do well on a test, and travel safely without using God. There are a lot of skinny, smart, living atheists. Please do not read this book (or the Bible for that matter) to see only what you can get from God. The good news of the gospel is not what we can use God to get but that we can get God. Let me say that again. *We can get God.* In all of his glory, all of his goodness, all of his love, grace, forgiveness, and truth, we are offered everything God is in relationship with him. We are offered this not merely as spectators or adherents to a religion but as adopted children of a Father who loves us. Through Christ, we can be sons and daughters of God in a right relationship with him. That's amazing.

This starts with God, not us. So let's start with God. I don't want you to read this as coming from a lecture podium or ivory tower. I am struggling with many of these ideas and applications as well. So I want to approach you as simply another weary traveler on life's path, looking at the map God has given that leads us straight to his heart. I want to have the conversation with you I wish I could have had with Mark and so many like him. I want you to read this as though we are sitting down at your favorite local coffee shop and talking over two steaming cups, waiting for them to cool. Let's start there.

God is good. God is right. God is love. However, those things may look different than you think. Let's talk about that. I'm glad you're here.

CHAPTER 1

The God We Don't Believe In

Fill in this blank.

"I don't believe in a God who _____."

Think about it.

"I don't believe in a God who causes _____."

"I don't believe in a God who would allow _____."

"I don't believe in a God who hates _____."

You and I have probably heard this answered in many different ways.

I don't believe in a God who causes <u>cancer</u>.

I don't believe in a God who <u>would let a child die</u>.

I don't believe in a God who <u>would send someone to hell</u>.

I don't believe in a God who hates <u>things like homosexual practice or abortion</u>.

Why do we think this? Because if we were God, we would never let someone have cancer. We would never let a child die. We would never allow any weighty consequence of judgment. We would just let people be and do what they wish if we were God because deep down, that is what we want from God. That is the God we want.

I live in Oklahoma, a state very familiar with tragedy. On May 20, 2013, an F4-level tornado ripped through heavily populated towns just south of Oklahoma City. This tornado destroyed homes and businesses, and it took lives. Some of those lives were tragically taken as winds and debris ripped open the roof and knocked down walls of an elementary school in the middle of the day, killing those within.

A year after the tragedy, a documentary was released at the Warren Theater in Moore, Oklahoma. The Warren Theater was one of the businesses greatly ravaged by the storm. The movie was called *Where Was God?: Stories of Hope After the Storm.*

I was struck by this title—*Where Was God?* It is a question that creates immediate theological tension because it presupposes a few things. First it assumes there is a God. Secondly it presupposes that in times of difficult tragedy like devastating tornadoes, there is a perceived absence of God, meaning the God we believe in is either absent from, averse to, or in some way not evident in tragedy.

If something good happens, glory to God! But if something bad happens, where was God? What happened to God? Why didn't he reveal himself? Something must be wrong. Where was God?

This is striking because in some way it reveals the God we don't believe in. The assumption of the movie title is not a stretch. It is something we all feel. It is a question we all have asked. We know God is love. We know God has made promises. We trust God has plans. We believe he wants to prosper us and not to harm us, to give us hope and a future. God is love, and if God is love, then he won't _____.

Let me ask you this question: What if he did?

The way we answer questions like these reveals our views of God, the Bible, and ourselves. It also addresses deeper issues of how we view God in relation to reality. It reveals a line of faith that is different for each of us. The atheist may say, "I don't believe in a god at all. I draw my line of faith right here. Beyond this line, there is nothing."

Many people who call themselves *spiritual* may say, "I believe there's a god. I'll walk down a little further. I believe there is something or someone there. But I don't believe in a god who would send someone to hell. I don't believe in that kind of judgment. I draw my line here. I don't believe in that god."

Others may say, "Okay, I believe in a literal hell. I believe there is a judgment, but I don't believe there's only one way to get to God. That is way too exclusive. God is inclusive. Jesus Christ is the *only* way to get to God? I don't believe in that God. I'll take a few more steps, but I draw my line of faith right here." In other words, we will only extend our line of trust in God so far. Over that, either there is no God, or we think he is a chump and want nothing to do with him.

But what if there is still truth across that line? Understand that there are indeed lines of truth. There are things God is and God is not. These things never change. But what if we have drawn a line in our minds, hearts, and actions that leaves out a very deep, real, and good part of who God is? Would God be loving or unloving to reveal that to us? Would God be loving even if that revelation came through the _____ we listed previously?

When I was in tenth grade, I was very short for my age. I was also what some had described as "portly" or "rotund." These were the days of Nirvana. We grew out our hair as a means of thrashing out our teenage angst in rhythm to overly distorted four-chord songs, making sure everyone knew and heard how much we didn't care about what they knew or heard. As any good teenager did at that time, I had grown out my hair. I also had glasses that (no lie) were the same exact frames my sister had.

One day at school, we discovered one of our teachers was sick. She would be replaced by a substitute for the majority of the week. The sub seemed nice enough and quickly made friends in the classroom. I, however, was too shy, and in my introversion I stooped to avoid interaction. I sat at the back of the room in my chair and quietly drew with a sharpie on my backpack.

After three days with the substitute, I saw one of the more outgoing members of our class go up to him and ask a question. In their hushed tones, I was unable to hear what they were talking about, but I did hear the substitute's reply. He said, "Well, what about the little girl at the back?"

My classmate replied, "What girl?"

In order to clarify, the substitute looked back at my table, pointed his finger, and said, "That girl in the Oasis T-shirt" (Leave me alone. "Wonderwall" was a game changer). As I squirmed in my seat and felt the eyes of both the substitute and classmate falling upon me, I heard her say, "Ryan? That's a guy!" Then there was an awkward pause.

I will never forget the substitute's reply. While the majority of their conversation had been hushed and calm, the substitute, obviously caught off guard, yelled loudly, *"No way!"* The next day I got a haircut, went on a diet, and told my mom I needed contacts.

People had told me I should cut my hair. They had hir
me that I was wearing glasses suited for a teenage girl. The
implied that it might be profitable for me to lose a few pounds.
But as I said before, I didn't care. These were the days of Nirvana!
I smelled like teen spirit!

Did I ever want someone to think I was a girl? No. For three
days? No. But I'm glad I went through it. I learned from it. I
changed from it. I was corrected by it and grew from it.

This is obviously a very silly example, but hopefully it points
us to a very real truth. Sometimes we learn best in situations we
would never choose. So does God cause or give these situations
just so we will learn? Perhaps. I don't know. But I do know in
every one of these situations, God is at work, and God is good.
We need not presume his absence.

This book focuses on Jesus's work in John 11 to redefine
people's expectations of God. Before we go to John 11 or talk
about what Jesus does, I need to frustrate you. Our initial desire
at this point is to jump right in to John 11 and start fixing what
may be broken. Why waste any more time before we get to the
meat of the discussion?

However, if you were sitting down to do a puzzle, you
would want to know how many pieces are in the puzzle and
what the picture on the box looks like. These are basic puzzle-
solving parameters. We must have a degree of perspective and
order before we can begin snapping pieces together. Instead of
snapping all the pieces of John 11 into form, we need to first step
back and take a look at the big picture. We need to know from
and about whom we are hearing.

This brings us to the book of John. John is a simple guy. When I say simple, I don't mean that he is unintelligent or backwoodsy. I mean that he is very straightforward. He doesn't use complicated language. Introductory-level seminary Greek classes begin by translating the book of John. It is the easiest to translate.

Because John is a simple and straightforward guy, he gives us a simple and straightforward purpose statement for his writing. "Now Jesus did many other signs in the presence of the disciples, which are not written in this book; but these are written so that you may believe that Jesus is the Christ, the Son of God, and that by believing you may have life in his name" (John 20:30–31).

John uses several key words here, but I want to momentarily focus on one word—*signs*. John says he writes about these *signs* so that you, the reader, may believe. Believe what? Specifically that Jesus is the Christ, the Son of God, and that by believing, you may have life in his name. Simple.

John is writing a plea for us, the readers, to have life in the Son of God, the Christ, Jesus. He does so by structuring his book around seven main signs. These signs are important. As John says, this is how he is going to accomplish his goal. It is how he is going to convey the life-altering account of Jesus Christ.

John intersperses these signs with dialogue and explanation. Each of these seven signs reveals some specific characteristic of Jesus's power and person.

Before we go further, it will be important for us to consider what a sign is. This will give us a proper context to understand these particular signs. For example, no one is intimidated by a red metal octagon. In and of itself, it is relatively useless, though it certainly may draw attention. It is negligible. However, if we saw a red metal octagon raised on a metal pole next to the road, we would have a different response altogether. We would recognize that the sign is there with a unique purpose. At some point there would be enough evidence to assess that that particular area required notification for those entering it. In fact, it could be dangerous if left unchecked.

The presence of the stop sign represents a greater reality. Its weight is not found in its substance but in the reality it represents. It is the same with the signs of Jesus. While Jesus's signs were more intricate than a red metal octagon, their purpose was the same. Granted, people derived benefit and even joy from Jesus's signs. They were not negligible. They were amazing and miraculous. As we explore them, we may even be awed by them. However, if we merely treat them as great things in and of themselves, we will dangerously drive right past the sign and miss the gravity and notification it represents.

The first sign is given in John 2:1–11, where Jesus changes water into wine. As John notes, the water was meant for Jewish purification. The fact that Jesus turns it into wine is significant. This is a picture of Jesus coming to fulfill the Old Testament law. The water needed for purification is replaced by wine. John shows us at the Last Supper that wine is representative of Jesus's blood. It is a symbol of fellowship. Law has been changed to relationship.

Not only did Jesus make this elemental change from water to wine, but the people also raved that it was *good* wine. This showed a distinct purpose for Jesus's mission. Humans tried to clean themselves up in order to be presentable to God. Jesus would change (or fulfill) this. He himself would be the agent of purification. Community and life with him would be the means through which we come to God. Not only that, but it would be sweet. It would be good. The cup that Jesus gave would be good. Jesus instantly changed mere water into something that usually took months or years to make. Jesus did it instantly through a substitution. He is the master of purity and quality.

The second sign is the healing of the nobleman's son in John 4:46–54. In this account, Jesus heals a boy who is more than twenty miles away. This shows that Jesus is master over not only purity and quality but also distance and space. He is not bound by them but exceeds them.

The third sign is the healing of a sick man in John 5:1–9. This man had been an invalid for more than thirty-five years. Think about that. For thirty-five years this man had lived in a relatively incapacitated state. But that is no match for Jesus. Jesus reversed thirty-five years in an instant. He is the master over time and the status quo.

The fourth sign is the feeding of the five thousand in John 6:1–14. Jesus, facing an enormous crowd who had come to hear his teaching, takes two small loaves of bread and five small fish and feeds thousands. Not only are they fed, but they are also satisfied. Not only are they satisfied, but there is also more than they can eat. They receive more abundantly than they ever could have imagined. Jesus shows he is the master of provision.

The fifth sign John gives shows Jesus walking on water in John 6:16–21. Jesus shows he is the master over nature—defying the physical realm and understanding of the disciples.

As for the sixth sign, Jesus heals a man who was born blind in John 9:1–12. In doing so, he shows the disciples that he is the master over hardship, circumstance, and physical malady.

We like this God. We like the idea of a God who turns mere water into wine. We all celebrate the blessing of a few loaves of bread, and pieces of fish into a feast for thousands. We like a God who gives more than we can imagine and fixes our ills. We like the word *instantly.* It appeals to everything we want God to be and do for us.

Then we get to the seventh and last sign (though some consider the resurrection an eighth and final sign). This is the sign where we are going to press the pause button and then watch in slow motion. This is the miracle we may miss if we run by too quickly. In John 11:1–46, Jesus raises a man named Lazarus from the dead. He displays his authority and mastership over man's greatest enemy—death. But how he does it raises many questions about the God in whom we have placed our faith.

Remembering John's purpose for writing his entire book, we must remember the context in which each of the signs is given. These seven signs are all being used to point to who Jesus, the Christ, the Son of God, actually is. He is not bound by man's efforts, quality, distance, time, space, quantity, natural law, understanding, pain, disease, or hardship. Not even death can hold him because he is its master.

On paper these are things we would normally celebrate. Oddly enough, John shows us in reality they were not received well.

Author Merrill C. Tenney has broken down the fallout of these signs for us.[2] The first two signs create a period of consideration

(John 1:19–4:54) in which people ask, "Is this the Christ?" We see this in conversation between Jesus and Nicodemus, a prominent religious leader.[3] Then this question is raised after a controversial encounter with a Samaritan woman at a watering well. After an exposing and uncomfortable dialogue, she runs back to her town, saying, "Come, see a man who told me all that I ever did. *Can this be the Christ?*"

The next three signs, which are found in John 5:1–6:71, develop a period of controversy in which people attempt to step beyond the previous question of whether Jesus is the Christ and begin to wonder what kind of Christ he is.

This leads to the sixth and seventh signs, in which we are ushered into the period of crisis (John 11:54–12:36). In the period of crisis, people begin not to speculate about Jesus's deity or his purpose, but many conclude this man simply has to die. He is not being, doing, saying, controlling in the manner they expected of the Messiah. He doesn't look like the Savior.

From our vantage point, we can see Jesus is the Messiah. We know *they* are wrong, not *him*. But they cannot take the tension. As a result, they say it is better for one man to die than for their place, prominence, and security to be challenged. Jesus has to die.

So who is this God? He seems foreign to many of us. Words like *controversy, conflict,* and *crisis* are not words we often associate with God or the Christian life. These aren't our ABCs of Christianity. Christian bookstores don't sell a lot of children's pastel wall decorations that declare, "Jesus causes crisis!"

However, John clearly shows us that this is Jesus's purposeful, predetermined path to reveal the truth about himself. It is the best if not only path. John says simply, "This is who Jesus is." It is messy, but he wants you to believe the truth and have real life in Jesus by believing. This creates tension both for those in Jesus's time and for us. We will see this tension as we go through the text and unpack its meaning throughout the following chapters. We will respond in one of two ways. Either we will relent under the tension, or it will break us. There is ultimately no third option.

CHAPTER 2

The God Who Is

What if I told you I just saw a Vincent van Gogh painting? Well, your reaction would depend on where I saw it. If you knew I had recently been to a museum, this would be a relatively short conversation. However, if I had just come down from your attic, it would be a different scenario entirely.

What if I told you I just saw Kevin Durant? Your response and reaction would depend greatly on whether I just saw a highlight of him on ESPN or if he just walked by the coffee shop window.

To truly understand anything and react properly, we must know a very important thing—the context. Context is king. This is why in a book focusing on what Jesus teaches us about God as we walk through John 11, we still have not gotten to John 11. We must first see John 11 in the context of the book of John as a whole. More than that, we need to know the reason John is writing this account to us in this manner. What is he trying to stress to us, the readers?

We have already noted that John gives us his overarching reason for writing. This is the soil in which his words spring to life. "Now Jesus did many other signs in the presence of the disciples, which are not written in this book; but these are written so that you may believe that Jesus is the Christ, the Son of God, and that by believing you may have life in his name" (John 20:30–31).

John says, "I want you to know Jesus and in doing so, have life." Single guys, if I told you, "I want you to know Katy and in doing so, have a wonderful, amazing marriage," you would have questions. Who is Katy? Where is she from? What does she look like? How old is she? Introductions raise questions. John is introducing Jesus. This is why John is a book full of questions about Jesus.

John wants us to ask questions, but he does us a favor in giving us his purpose statement—that we may believe Jesus is the Christ, the Son of God, and by believing we may have life in his name. But knowing there are questions about Jesus (and knowing this process is a journey), John sets out with a very purposeful, beautiful, haunting, poetic, overarching truth about who Jesus is. He does this so as the people in these accounts are wondering, we don't have to wonder. They question, and we know the answer. We may not like the answer or how it is revealed, but John sets the context for the whole book (including chapter 11) in John 1:1–18.

Just as I gave you an introduction to this book to frame the best way of reading and understanding what is ahead, John gives us an introduction to his book. This prologue in essence is not just a synopsis of the entire book but the entire theology and salvation history of the Bible. Let's read it together to discover who Jesus is. "In the beginning was the Word, and the Word was with God, and the Word was God. He was in the beginning with

God. All things were made through him, and without him was not any thing made that was made" (John 1:1–3).

I could write volumes on just these words. But with his goal in mind, John establishes first that before anything was, God, the Word, the Logos, *was*. The Greek word used here literally means "He always was continuing." *The Word* was and is Jesus's continuing identity from all eternity. He was God constantly.

Look around you. Think, feel, smell, and listen. Before any of this, the Word was. He was in the beginning. He was with God (note the Trinitarian language), and he was God.

And who is he? He is the Creator. "All things were made through him" (John 1:3). John is extremely clear here. Regardless of how intolerant, exclusive, divisive, offensive, or closed-off this may seem, not only does John establish that all things were made through Jesus, the Word, but in case there was any doubt, he goes a step further. Lest there be any confusion, John says that not only were all things made through him but that "without him was not any thing made that was made." Drop the mic.

This truth is not unique to John. Let's take a look at this throughout Scripture. "For by him all things were created, in heaven and on earth, visible and invisible, whether thrones or dominions or rulers or authorities—all things were created through him and for him. And he is before all things, and in him all things hold together" (Colossians 1:16–17). "In these last days God has spoken to us by his Son, whom he appointed the heir of all things, through whom also he created the world. He is the radiance of the glory of God and the exact imprint of his nature, and he upholds the universe by the word of his power" (Hebrews 1:2–3). "Worthy are you, our Lord and God, to receive glory and honor and power, for you created all things, and by your will they existed and were created" (Revelation 4:11).

By beginning in this way, John is establishing something important about Jesus. Jesus has the credentials. He has the authority.

Charles Steinmetz was a mechanical genius and a friend of Henry Ford, the inventor of the automobile assembly line. It was said of Steinmetz that he could build a motor in his mind, and if it broke, he could fix it in his mind before he ever touched it.

One day the assembly line at Ford's plant broke down. Ford called in all his best and brightest engineers. Sadly none of them could fix it. At last he called Steinmetz. The mechanical genius looked at it, tinkered with it a few minutes, and then threw the switch, and it started running again. Good as new.

A few days later, Ford received a bill from Steinmetz for $10,000. Ford wrote back and said, "Charlie, don't you think that is a bit high for just a little tinkering?"

Steinmetz sent back a revised bill that said, "Tinkering—$10. Knowing where to tinker—$9,990."

Charles Steinmetz could work on your engine because he thought of it, made it, knows how it works, and knows how to use it. God rules over all because he thought of it, made it, and knows how it works and how to use it. Many people in our society today believe that they can tinker with what God has established, that somehow it's fluid and subject to their whim and mercy. But only God has the authority. Only God has the right. Only God has the credentials.

"In him was life, and the life was the light of men. The light shines in the darkness, and the darkness has not overcome it"

(John 1:4–5). John is beginning his book and establishing Jesus by introducing two themes. In fact, as you read through the book of John, it is a fun idea to circle or underline every time the words *light* or *life* are mentioned. These two ideas continue to come up in the book of John in some amazing ways that allude to the truths of Jesus Christ.

Light. Where light goes, it dispels darkness. Darkness is the absence of light. Where it exists, there can be no darkness. Light is the revealing agent of truth. John says Jesus is the light, the revealing agent of truth to all men. John MacArthur notes,

> John is writing that life and light cannot be separated. They are essentially the same, with the idea of light emphasizing the manifestation of the divine life. "The life was the light" is the same construct as "the Word was God" (v.1). As God is not separate from the Word, but the same in essence, so life and light share the same essential properties. Light and life are linked in this same way in John 8:12 in which Jesus says: "I am the Light of the world; he who follows me will not walk in the darkness, but will have the Light of life."[4]

John continues this transcendent metaphor. "The true light, which gives light to everyone, was coming into the world. He was in the world, and the world was made through him, yet the world did not know him. He came to his own, and his own people did not receive him" (John 1:9–11).

In a way this is John's Christmas narrative—his description of the hypostatic union, the Word made flesh. Light was coming into the world he made. This is the very world that he is Creator of and Lord over. Tragically this world did not know him.

This isn't a "who is that?" type of not knowing. It is not an ignorance of facts. There are many people you know but very few you truly *know*. They refused him. As Isaiah says, "He was despised and rejected by men" (Isaiah 53:3). He held authority, and they mocked him. They did not interact or relate intimately with God. God gave the Way. They chose to try to forge a different path.

John says that when Jesus came, he came with such a force that not reacting was not an option. In Matthew 16, Jesus asks his disciples, "How are they reacting? Who do they say that I am?" Some said John the Baptist. Others said Elijah, Jeremiah, or a prophet. Today some say Jesus is a good teacher, a narcissistic Zeus, or a disinterested clockmaker. Some say he is a hate monger, a bigot, a pretty boy, or a right-winger. To some, he is a sugar daddy, a pushover, a weak cosmic Santa Claus. He's something we reference like the universe or Mother Nature. He's a nice thought but mentioned with a wink like parents talking about the Easter bunny around their kids. He's harmless. He's enabling. He's weak.

Jesus says, "But who do you say that I am?" Simon Peter replied, "You are the Christ, the Son of the living God." Jesus answered, "Blessed are you, Simon [son of] Jonah! For flesh and blood has not revealed this to you, but my Father who is in heaven" (Matthew 16:17).

> And the Word became flesh and dwelt among us, and we have seen his glory, glory as of the only Son from the Father, full of grace and truth … For from his fullness

we have all received grace upon grace. For the law was given through Moses; grace and truth came through Jesus Christ. No one has ever seen God; the only God, who is at the Father's side, he has made him known. (John 1:14–18)

Not only did God come to us, but he openly, unapologetically, unabashedly, no-holds-barred showed and revealed himself to us. His character, truth, knowledge, and life are made known to us. We have seen his glory as only he could give it, full of grace and truth. We have seen God. We can know God in and through Jesus Christ. Stop and consider what a miracle this is. We do not need another miracle. We can know God. We don't have to guess or live in the fear of uncertainty. We don't have to struggle with trying to make the pieces fit, clawing our way to a deity in the dark. He came to us. And he is good and full of truth and grace upon grace.

I love that phrase "grace upon grace." It is a word picture that reminds me of a restaurant in the Dallas area called Babe's. Babe's serves family style Southern comfort food. You simply order a few items, and they keep bringing more of them. You're getting low on potatoes? Here are some hot ones. How are we on chicken fingers? Good? Well, we've got more. Here is more—heap upon heap. The only thing they don't give you more of is the pie because you would literally kill yourself eating pie, and it would be marvelous.

John gives this word picture of continually replacing, never running dry—heap upon heap, grace upon grace. We can never exhaust his grace. Why is this? Because we don't supply it. It is not doled out unconsciously or with reserve. It is because of the cross. Jesus paid it all. It is enough. It's not about how much grace you can earn because it doesn't come from you. It comes from God. We know this because *he* became flesh. *He* dwelt among us. We have seen *his* glory as the only Son from the Father, full of grace and truth. We never would have known. But God himself has made him known.

John says from the outset this is the God we are dealing with. This is not the one we made up or want. This is the one that *is*. This is how he reveals himself. Certainly this involves questions, signs, and difficult truths. Some are going to love him. Some are going to hate him. But as John unfolds the truth that Jesus reveals, the tension between those who love him, tolerate him, or hate him grows more and more—until it snaps in John 11.

So this is our context. It is the puzzle board and the pieces. This is where we are going to be throughout the chapters that follow. As we begin, it is important that we set the context and seek to gain an understanding. God is God even if in reality he is and has revealed himself to be the God we don't believe in.

John has established his goal for writing. He wants us to know Jesus and have life in his name. He has introduced us to the Christ, the Word made flesh. These are great concepts and truths. But what do these concepts look like when they are pounded against the pavement of reality? In John 11, we will see what happens when Jesus's priority of God's eternal glory grates against mankind's expectation of temporal and expedient satisfaction.

As we walk together, we will see the following ways in which Jesus reveals the reality of God in John 11. We will see the God who waits (John 11:1–6), the God who gives doubt (John 11:7–16), the God who loses (John 11:17–37), the God who raises the dead (John 11:38–44), and the God who creates tension (John 11:45–12:11).

You may be someone or know someone who says, "God would never wait. God would never allow grief or pain. I don't believe in a God who gives doubt. God doesn't lose, raise the dead or create tension."

Get ready. I am grateful you are reading this book. I am happy to be walking this road with you. "These are written so that you may believe that Jesus is the Christ, the Son of God, and that by believing you may have life in his name" (John 20:30–31).

CHAPTER 3

The God Who Waits

We have all had to wait. It is a part of being human. It is the kick in the pants of living in time. Some things like waiting for a green light, the release of the next Apple device, or that annoying extra second for a website to load are relatively inconsequential. They are more of an annoyance than anything. Some things we wait for have a much greater gravity.

The difficult thing about waiting for big things is that we tend to transition at some point from hoping a reality will happen to *assuming* the reality will happen. When it does not materialize, it is no longer the validity of our hopes that comes into question but the means through which we assumed those hopes would come. We've been robbed. It is someone or something else's fault. There was a truth and a reality, and something cheated us of it. We have been hurt. We want answers.

When I was a young teenager, my grandpa gave me opportunities to learn about hard work, discipline, follow-through, and responsibility. To a teenager, those are cuss words. On weekends my dad and grandpa set up opportunities for me to work around my grandpa's house. Looking back on it, the jobs were relatively easy, and the pay was good. Mostly I would mow his lawn and wash his cars. My grandpa had a gray Buick town car and a big blue Chevy truck. Each weekend I would wash them, and he would inspect them. I would get paid based on how well I performed.

One particular day as I was cleaning off dead bugs from the grill of the Buick, my grandpa came out and sat under a nearby tree. He didn't talk. He seemed to have no real purpose for being out there other than enjoying the day and watching me wash the car. I assumed he was merely keeping an eye on the process and wanted to make sure I was doing a good job. So I kept washing.

After I had finished, my grandpa called me over to sit in the shade with him. We small talked for a while, but it quickly became apparent we weren't there to talk about clean cars.

I hadn't noticed the headaches. I didn't know about the fainting spells. The mixed up words and instances of confusion to me were just signs that grandpa was getting old. After all, who didn't forget a few things every once in a while?

I was being sheltered by a family who loved me, but we had apparently reached a point where ignorance was no longer an option. My grandpa had a brain tumor. It was growing, and successful treatment options were not probable. My grandpa was one of the strongest men I had ever known. He told me he was going to beat cancer. He said *we* were going to beat this. He just wanted me to know and not be afraid. We would win.

What I didn't know at that point was the doctors had given my grandpa about six months to live. Even that was optimistic. We watched as his eyesight failed, his words slurred, and his clothes began to hang from his withering body. For two years my grandpa's body fought against the enemy within, and as a young teen, I watched one of my great heroes die. My parents no longer sheltered me. I helped my dad change my grandpa's diapers. I helped give him his medicine. I transitioned from washing and cleaning his cars to washing and tending to his bedsores. We were not going to win.

I distinctly remember sitting on my bathroom floor the morning of his funeral. I think this was the first time I had really felt hurt by God. Life had thrown its share of rocks, and I had come to God to nurse bruises; however, this was different. Our family needed my grandpa. Why take him so young? Why hold out the promise of healing? What is the purpose of hope if its pedestal is already occupied by fate? I had waited for healing. Now I was waiting for answers.

John's main goal in writing his book is that we may know who Jesus is and have life in his name. What we see repeatedly throughout the gospel is people encountering life in Christ and not wanting it. It is uncomfortable. It is different than what they had believed. A believable lie—though certainly a lie—is still believable. Jesus came so that we might reject the believable lie we want and embrace the unbelievable truth we need.

This is a believable lie: God cares too much for us to wait. God loves us, so he won't let us feel hurt or disappointment. When we do engage hurt, questions, or disappointment, other questions arise. If we have to wait, maybe God doesn't love us. Maybe we aren't even Christians. Maybe we haven't performed to a high enough level or shown enough faith. Or to a greater degree, maybe God isn't as intimately involved in our lives as we had thought. At times we may use this as an excuse to sin. After all, if God is going to be distant, then he won't care if we do this. Perceived distance becomes a reason to distance ourselves further. What good is prayer if we aren't going to get what we ask for? What good is God if he doesn't come through when we need him most? I've sung the songs, hung the Scripture passages on my wall, watched every Veggie Tales movie, but maybe the God I was all hyped up about simply is not that God.

That is a believable lie. Jesus shows us an unbelievable truth, namely that we serve a God who waits, and that is a good thing.

> Now a certain man was ill, Lazarus of Bethany, the village of Mary and her sister Martha. It was Mary who anointed the Lord with ointment and wiped his feet with her hair, whose brother Lazarus was ill. So the sisters sent to him, saying, "Lord, he whom you love is ill." But when Jesus heard it he said, "This illness does not lead to death. It is for the glory of God, so that the Son of God may be glorified through it." Now Jesus loved Martha and her sister and Lazarus. So, when he heard that Lazarus was ill, he stayed two days longer in the place where he was. (John 11:1–6)

In the opening two verses of our text, John offers some basic biographical information as a canvas upon which he will paint the unfolding scene. One of the first things he notes is that Lazarus and his sisters were in the town of Bethany. Bethany was about two miles east of Jerusalem—a suburb of sorts—on the way to Jericho toward the Jordan River. Jesus spent a lot of time in Bethany. His acts there would come to define the city. In fact, today the town is called El-Azariyeh, meaning "the Town of Lazarus."

John introduces not only the location of the event but the major characters as well. We know Mary and Martha mostly from Luke 10 in their famous discussion about how to serve Jesus. We will discuss that in more detail later. While that is how we think of Mary initially, John points to a different scene for us to recall. He notes, "It was Mary who anointed the Lord with ointment and wiped his feet with her hair." Interestingly enough, John doesn't record Mary doing this until later in chapter 12. Apparently Mary was so shaped by the Lazarus event that her act of worship in response became the key way in which she was known to her contemporaries.

John takes care to note that Mary, Martha, and Lazarus are close to Jesus. They are not merely followers, but they are loved by Jesus in a unique way. When Mary and Martha send word to Jesus, they do so under a banner of relationship. They are reminding Jesus of his deep care for Lazarus by simply calling him "he whom you love." There is no greater plea or direction. They believe simply informing Jesus will be enough. Their faith in him to come and to do the right thing is directly implied.

Mary and Martha are calling on Jesus not just as the Son of God but as a personal friend. Lazarus is sick. There is a deep sense of desperation. The message from Mary and Martha is emotionally loaded. They are not just people in the crowd. They are friends. The least Jesus can do is come for them. If strangers are healed by merely touching him, surely friends will receive a greater and swifter response.

They know who Jesus is. They know what he can do. They trust him to do it. However, trusting is one thing. Walking on that trust like a tightrope is different. Frederick Bruner reminds us,

> This is how petitioners experience Jesus often enough to be deeply discouraged. The Lord's timing, let us admit, does not always seem good. We readers know the end of this story and so have some relief; but this hurting family (and every other hurting family before and since) does not know future particulars at all and so is very vulnerable. Jesus' delays always hurt. Our text is honest.[5]

I'm glad the Bible is honest. It shows me Mary and Martha were presuming on Jesus and imploring Jesus the way he tells us to implore him. We are to trust God as a good Father who will not give a stone when we ask for bread. We are told to entreat him like a persistent widow imploring a king to work on her behalf. We are told to trust him more than the sparrows that do not worry about food, clothing, or investment portfolios.

When Mary and Martha send the messengers to Jesus, they must have continually kept an eye on Lazarus. Who knows how Jesus would respond? Maybe he will know their faith and heal Lazarus before the messengers even get there, showing the glory of his foreknowledge. Knowing it would take a day for the messengers to get there, they probably woke up the day after sending the message expectant as the man who found out his son had been healed despite great distance (John 4:46-54). Jesus will come through any moment now. What a great opportunity for Jesus to do a miracle and manifest his glory. They must have watched Lazarus get sicker and sicker while they still kept one eye out the window, waiting for the figure of Jesus to penetrate the horizon.

So where was Jesus? Jesus was in another familiar place. John tells us he was beyond the Jordan. He had gone out to the place where John the Baptist used to baptize. Mary and Martha likely knew where he was. He had retreated to that place after a narrow escape from the crowd in Jerusalem who sought to stone him for blasphemy, specifically for claiming to be God.

It is there the messengers find him after about a day and relay the burning message. Jesus's response is exactly what they want to hear. It is a promise of victory, a proclamation of triumph. "This illness does not lead to death. It is for the glory of God, so that the Son of God may be glorified through it" (John 11:4).

The messengers must have exhaled a sigh of relief. Their hope was secured. Though tired from a long journey, they likely dashed back toward Bethany, reenergized by the message of victory and life they would soon deliver to the sisters.

"This illness does not lead to death." For those of us who know the rest of the story, this is where we get uncomfortable with Jesus. Yes, it does. It does lead to death. Lazarus is going to die ... and soon. It is likely the messengers who ran back to the two waiting sisters with a message of hope and secure faith in Jesus as the Christ crossed the threshold to find the sisters mourning and Lazarus's body lying still. No movement. No breath. No life. This illness had led to death.

Can you imagine the mind-set of the messengers at this point? Certainly they had not misheard Jesus. They had a promise from the lips of Jesus Christ himself. They carried back a great message of life and hope. But as they ran back into the house, their joy, hope, security, and confidence in Jesus collapsed to the ground like the dust behind their feet.

We read these words and sense the joy in the messengers, sisters, and disciples, but at the back of our minds, we are bothered. Even if we want to give Jesus the benefit of the doubt, this seems manipulative. It seems uncaring, mean, misleading. It doesn't seem ... Christlike.

But if we are in the shoes of the disciples, not knowing the condition of Lazarus, this is where Jesus fills our mold to bursting measure. It is where he dons the cape, pulls off the glasses, and reveals the Superman Jesus we want him to be. Jesus comes to the rescue!

This is where we often land with Jesus. We read verses of bold promise. We write them on our mirrors, embroider them on our pillows, and print them on our coffee mugs. We hold to the words that we want to hear (though they are taken out of the context of unique persons and situations and often deceptively applied to us). God has a plan for us to prosper, to give us hope and a future. Nothing will separate us from the love of God. All things work for our good. If God is for us, who can be against us? Death has no sting. Victory! This illness will not lead to death. We put the cape on God.

Then we turn on the news. We take another pill on another morning when waking up seems like an unwarranted necessity. Our loved ones still reject Christ. Our neighbors get sick. We feel the weight of sin in the world. Violence grows, and people raise the banner of progress over a decaying and regressive world.

Sometimes it seems to be a Christian, you have to close your eyes, shut the windows, stick your fingers in your ears, and repeat, "Hallelujah, hallelujah, hallelujah," until it starts to warp your worldview into a false utopia the rest of the world stands to mock. This illness often leads to death.

How could it be that Lazarus's illness would not end in death? Because we and God often have different definitions of *end*. God's perspective begins and ends with his *shalom*, his peace, his rightness that was established in the garden of Eden, and it is realized in Revelation 21–22. To Jesus, Lazarus's death was a parenthesis in his greater story. In fact, the greater story wasn't about Lazarus at all. Rather it was the part he was to play in the unfolding glory and revelation of God.

What greater way could Jesus love Lazarus than to use him in the revealing of God's glory? Is there any greater end for us? Again, our answer to this question relies on our definition of *end*. Our perspective on God, life, circumstance, joy, sorrow, pain, and peace will greatly depend on whether we see ourselves as an end or a means.

Culture is bent on telling us what we deserve—that we are the ends. We are the consumers. Their products are the means to our greatest end, whatever that may be. For some it is health, wealth, happiness, security, or an escape. But let's be honest. We are all just one phone call away from those straw fortresses being toppled and exposed for what they are.

Jesus loves us too much to let us hide in straw fortresses. The only firm and strong tower is God himself. Only he knows truth, can provide righteousness, and can provide salvation from the greatest enemy, sin, which leads to a spiritual and eternal death apart from Christ. Will your sickness lead to death? Not for those in Christ Jesus.

"Now Jesus loved Martha and her sister and Lazarus. So, when he heard that Lazarus was ill, he stayed two days longer in the place where he was" (John 11:5–6).

John wants us to understand the love of God. He is quick to point out after the confusing words of Christ that Jesus loved not only Lazarus, who was ill, but also Martha and her sister, Mary. Love is the bridge between the promise of life and the delay of God. Jesus loves them, so he waits.

Not only does he wait, but he waits two days. This is significant. Consider the fact that the messengers would take one day to get to Jesus, and once he set out, it would take a day for Jesus and the disciples to travel. Jesus adds to these two days of traveling necessity two days of delay. His plan is to arrive four days late.

Was this easy for Jesus? I don't know. I want to think the delay of God is excruciating for him as he watches me wait in the dark. However, I know to God this is a purposeful stretching of faith and growth. This is the working out of his love. This is a loving Father giving his child the greatest gift—himself. This is the glory of God. Westcott notes, "Because the Lord loved the family He went at the exact moment when His visit would be most fruitful and not just when He was invited."[6] Jesus loved Martha, her sister, and Lazarus, so he stayed where he was for two more days. As C. S. Lewis once said, "I am sure God keeps no one waiting unless He sees that it is good for him to wait."[7]

How are we supposed to feel about this? What is your reaction to the God who waits? We may have initial undercurrents of sadness, anger, or unfairness. We understand that this is God is and that he is doing what is best. But if he is God, couldn't he do it another way? Does God expect us simply to be resigned to this idea? When will God make himself glorious through good things?

We've been there. Consider the business opportunity that you had to keep putting on the back burner and eventually fell through. Does God not want us to provide for his church and our family?

The relationship was strained or even broken when we tried to do the right thing—the gospel thing. Could God not have just changed their hearts?

The illness keeps us sidelined in the battle we want to fight.

Consider the circumstance we can't get out of but just want to put behind us. We wait. And we wait. We watch opportunity after opportunity for God to work in the way we believe he should pass by into the wind, forgotten.

I have a lot of plans for God. I have a general understanding of who he is, what he can do, and why he wants to do it. When I am in a position of waiting, I like to think my instinct is to say, "Whatever God wills." If I am honest, while those may be the words on my lips, the attitude in my heart says, "What do I need to do? What have I not done?"

We expect God to do what we would do. But we aren't God. In fact, that is a good thing—a great blessing to humanity. We really don't make the best decisions, and the decisions we do make are often self-serving.

It is easy to accept that truth with a sly, self-effacing smirk. But on the big questions of timing and life's big decisions, we often think we are the preeminent decision makers. We have put in the time. We have weighed the pros and cons. We've thought this through. In fact, wouldn't we just be doing God a favor by not bothering him (you know, with all of his needing to keep the entire universe existing) and giving him the bullet points on the situation and a general recommended plan of action for him to follow?

The problem with that is we often think through circumstances and issues with a certain end in mind. God has also thought them through with a certain end in mind. In fact, he did so before he spoke the world into being. However, if those ends are different, we will be pushing in divergent directions. This will create tension. The way we respond to that tension defines much of our worldview. We assume God's salvation, love, and protection will be manifested in certain ways. We sing about them and write them on our keepsakes, but are those God's ways or simply the ways we plan to use God in order to bring about the ends we believe are best?

The difficult thing about a God who waits is that he is still God. Being God, he has a far greater perspective, understanding, vantage point, and ability to order the world in a way that will bring about what is best. Not only that, but he truly knows what is best. Being a good and loving God, he gives that to us—grace upon grace—but he does so in accordance with a ranked set of priorities.

The difficult thing for us to accept is that God is the one who ranks those priorities. They are in accordance with the way reality is, the way he created it, the way it functions in truth. When we think of God waiting, there are three things from John

11:1–6 we can understand about God and his priorities that may help us wait with gospel-centered patience (and maybe even joy).

First God waits because he has a plan. Jesus was very intentional. He was obedient to the plan of God. Continually we are told Jesus is doing what he sees the Father doing and is acting so that the Scriptures may be fulfilled. Consider the reason Jesus is out in the desert when the messengers go to find him. Why not just get arrested in Jerusalem in John 10 and start the process of the cross? Jesus waits to die at the right time. That was his highest priority, the reason he came—to die the death we could not die and by his power, grace, and justice, raise us with himself on the third day.

In accordance with that, Jesus has a plan for everyone's lives and how *they* fit into *his* plan. There's the rub. Mary, Martha, and Lazarus could not possibly have understood the role they were playing in the redemptive salvation story of Jesus Christ. They could not have foreseen the foreshadowing and demonstration of Jesus's power over death that Lazarus's physical demise would play. At the time it may have looked like Jesus was letting Lazarus die in order to save his own life. Interestingly enough, it is Lazarus being brought to life that secures the verdict of death over Jesus. Lazarus's death was a step on the road of Jesus's power being displayed over life. Lazarus being raised to life was a step on Jesus's path to die on the cross.

Lazarus got sick before Jesus planned to go to Jerusalem. For Mary, Martha, and him, this seemed like an end, a final verdict. Jesus knew it was merely a subplot, a footnote in a much greater story. God's plan was to bring salvation to the whole world. Jesus did not stay because he wasn't compassionate or loving. Rather he stayed because his plan was best. Only he knew the bigger picture. God waits because he has a plan.

Secondly we need to understand God's plan is for God's glory. His glory is his greatest priority. It is the end. Everything else is the means. So what do we mean when we talk about the glory of God? What is it? That is a difficult question. It is almost as big as asking who God is in and of himself. When Moses asked God this question, he gave his name. He simply said, "I Am." *I am God. I was God. I will be God. I will always keep being and have constantly been God. I Am who I Am.* Because this is such a big question, we are going to need to spend a decent amount of time discussing it.

What is God's glory? It is not merely what God does or does not do. It is not simply his name in lights. God's glory is the essence of God himself. MacArthur notes, "The most important theme in the universe is the glory of God. It is the underlying reason for all of God's works, from the creation of the world, to the redemption of fallen sinners, to the judgment of unbelievers, to the manifestation of His greatness for all eternity in heaven."[8]

Understanding the centrality of God's glory is integral to understanding God's story of redemption. In case you are hesitant about the centrality of God's glory to his nature, consider the following snapshot of God's glory in Scripture. The Bible refers to God as

- the God of glory (Psalm 29:3; Acts 7:2),
- the glory of Israel (1 Samuel 15:29),
- the King of glory (Psalm 24:7–10),
- God the Father ... the Father of glory (Ephesians 1:17; 2 Peter 1:17),

- God the Son ... the Lord of glory (1 Corinthians 2:8),
- God the Holy Spirit ... the Spirit of glory (1 Peter 4:14), and
- God [who] will not share his glory with another (Isaiah 42:8; 48:11).

King David the psalmist proclaimed, "Be exalted above the heavens, O God; let Your glory be above all the earth" (Psalm 108:5).

King Solomon, a man filled with wisdom, exclaimed, "Blessed be His glorious name forever; and may the whole earth be filled with his glory" (Psalm 72:19).

The psalms rejoice in the glory of God as being "above the heavens" (Psalm 113:4). They exalt, "Great is the glory of the Lord" (Psalm 138:5), and they say, "His glory is above earth and heaven" (Psalm 148:13).

God's glory is revealed and displayed in his creation. The Bible declares, "The heavens are telling of the glory of God; and their expanse is declaring the work of His hands" (Psalm 19:1). "The whole earth is full of His glory" (Isaiah 6:3).

"His invisible attributes, His eternal power and divine nature, have been clearly seen" in his creation (Romans 1:20). God's judgment falls on those who reject his glory (Romans 1:22–23).

God is holy. His glory is even displayed in his judgment of fallen angels and fallen men (Exodus 14:4, 17–18). God saved sinners "to make known the riches of His glory upon vessels of mercy, which He prepared beforehand for glory" (Romans 9:23). "This salvation," Paul states, is "the gospel of the glory of Christ" (2 Corinthians 4:4).

God's action in salvation is ultimately for his own glory. Paul tells the church at Ephesus God predestined us to adoption as sons through Jesus Christ to Himself, according to the kind intention of His will, to the praise of the glory of His grace, which He freely bestowed on us in the Beloved (Ephesians 1:5–6; cf. vv. 12, 14, 18).

As God sanctifies sinners and the Holy Spirit pushes us toward Christ, we are filled "with the fruit of righteousness which comes through Jesus Christ, to the glory and praise of God" (Philippians 1:11; cf. John 15:8).

If you want to see the fullest and most gracious exhibition of God's glory, look no further than the coming of the Son of God, the Lord Jesus Christ, "the Word [who] became flesh, and dwelt among us, and we saw His glory, glory as of the only begotten from the Father, full of grace and truth" (John 1:14).[9] As Timothy Keller states, "When we look at Jesus Christ as he is shown to us in the Scriptures, we are looking at the glory of God through the filter of a human nature."[10]

God's glory is a big deal. It is the epicenter of the Bible. It is the gospel. If you miss it, you will miss the gospel. If you do not seek it, you will not seek the things of God. If you do not love and desire it, you will have no love or desire for God. God is displayed in his glory, and his glory is central to all things.

Before we go any further, we need to take a brief detour to set a very important definition. We need to talk about God's glory and the *gospel*.

The Bible tells us all we need to know to create an accurate worldview centered on God's glory. Some would shudder at the phrase "accurate worldview," as we increasingly attempt to legitimize a vast array and variety of worldviews, often affirming competing and mutually exclusive ones. This is the spiritual schizophrenia of our age. It is easy, however, to simply pass it off as an error of *our* age. In fact, this has been the error from the beginning.

"In the beginning God created the heavens and earth." That is how the Bible opens. There was a beginning for the heavens and earth. There was a God who preexisted everything he created. He created it with order and purpose. Most importantly, he created *it*. What is *it*? It is reality. It is the effulgence of God's glory. It is what fixes the skies apart from the dust, the wet from the dry, the animal from the plant, and the man from the animal.

In other words, God created boundaries. All of these boundaries served to create a reality in which certain things are and certain things are not. Not only are these physical realities, but they are also the realities of role, purpose, design, and function. Relationship, authority, love, gravity, emotion—all of these had a setting, and the setting was very good.

If we can think of reality as the 12:00 point on a watch dial, when Satan came to subvert that reality, he did not come at the 6:00 point. He did not try to convince Eve that the God they believed they saw was an apparition. He did not come with a humanistic apologetic or outline of Darwin's theories. Continuing the watch analogy, Satan didn't come at 6:00 to subvert the noonday sun. He came at 12:01, saying the sun was indeed in position. But maybe it was just a bit different than we thought. Not only that, but maybe we could alter it.

"Did God really say?" and "If this happens, surely this won't happen" were the arrows of Satan's earth-shattering quiver.

They've been rippling throughout time ever since, and he has chuckled at our numerous perversions of the reality that exists. But that's the problem. Reality still exists. Our continual struggle of bending the world to orbit on our own trajectory is what creates the great tensions of our souls. The Bible is basically the unfolding story of what reality is, how the view of it was splintered, and how we continually attempt to draw our own lines of reality either near or far from the way, the truth, and the life. Our custom is to validate individuals in their view of reality, no matter how dangerous or tension-creating it may be. This is the great error of man.

In his grace, God gave us the law—the outline of how reality still functions even in a fallen world. But its purpose was not to get us to morally walk the realistic line. Rather it was to show us that, like a staggering drunk man, we cannot walk the line though our lives depend on it. There is something in us that is wrong. We are infected with sin. Jesus entered a broken world and walked that line perfectly. We killed him for it. As God is a just judge, there must be a penalty for our cosmic treason. God paid it in the willing sacrifice of Jesus Christ, the God-man. He paid the monstrous debt mankind owed that only a perfect and blameless deity could pay.

Jesus paid this price and saved us from the weight of guilt around our necks. Those in Christ Jesus have been saved. He also gave us the Spirit who guides us toward being Christlike. The Holy Spirit is the voice that calls behind us when we turn to the right or the left, revealing to us the nature of our teacher and the joy of walking in reality. Those in Christ Jesus are being saved. Ultimately the Bible tells us that God will destroy error, the temptation from it and the penalty of it and that he will restore the world to existing in and enjoying this reality. Those in Christ Jesus will be saved.

The Bible also tells us God set his invisible attributes in his creation. When we enjoy the life found in reality and its goodness, we are actually enjoying the mirrored and manifest nature of God who displays his goodness in the reality he created. This rightness (righteousness) is actually one way we enjoy God. It is a way of worshipping him. All that is given to reflect and enjoy God ultimately serves to point to God and the beautiful person he is, the eternal Father, Son, and Spirit. This is the glory of God. It's simply God being God.

Jesus focused on one main priority—God's glory. Simply put, Jesus came to show God being God in every situation. His goal, as he said many times, was to bring glory to the Father. As Jesus saw the Father doing, so he did. He was God and was the exact representation of God. As John said, in the beginning was the Word (Jesus), and the Word was God. He was in the beginning with God. Jesus shows us God being God. This is the glory of God. This is the gospel.

For some this is easy to believe and assent to—that is, until the circumstance is a difficulty or trial. It is the tension of Jesus acting toward a goal contrary to our end goal. This is what was happening while John 11 was unfolding. Jesus was ranking values.

There is a long list of reasons Jesus needs to go to Lazarus right away. However, they are human reasons. They are human expectations. Jesus does not act in human terms but divine terms. They are of greater priority. There is one item on Jesus's list—the glory of God. This is good.

re is where the rubber meets the road for the believer. This is why we spent such length discussing the gospel, lines, reality, salvation, priority, and tension. The significance for the one who trusts in Jesus as the only way, truth, and life is that Jesus offers us great freedom in walking in the reality and joy of God's glory. Because Jesus was focused on divine priority and not human priority, he was free to do what God wanted, not what man wanted.

Note that Jesus is free from human expectations. As a follower of Jesus, you are free from human expectations. As a Christian, your life has been redeemed. This means you have a distinct purpose. There is one thing on your list. You must glorify God. The ways and means will look different for each of us. The Bible tells us how we glorify God as a man, husband, worker, wife, daughter, single adult, singer, mourner, accountant, etc. However, the expectation and the goal are the same.

This is the freedom of Christ. You do not have to create a reality. You do not have to be God. You cannot, and you are not. Read that again. Take a breath. Let that free you. You don't have the pressure on you to operate on a human level or to redefine humanity. You simply need to follow the voice of your shepherd. In doing so, the things you do will be aligned with what God is doing.

In reality, the only expectations on you are not human but divine. Things that are human fail. In fact, the Bible says they lead to death. They are destroyed by the weakest of things— moths and rust. Things that are divine never fail. We struggle and claw for fame, prosperity, reputation, and a kingdom that reflects us and points to our glory.

Friend, take that yoke off. When you look at divine expectations, you don't have to succumb to human expectations. Jesus's rightness (righteousness) is given to you in a divine transfer—your debt for his grace. Follow him in it. That's your purpose.

This brings us to the third and most penetrating attribute of God displayed in Jesus's choice to wait. By relying on his timing and not ours, this is how Jesus loves us. God waits because he loves us. He loves us with his glory. This is good. This is best.

Paul Maxwell explains, "First, if God didn't want a deep and affectionate relationship with you, he would give you everything you wanted immediately. He would placate you with the pleasures of this world. For those who know God, that is intuitively unlike him—not unlike him to bless, but unlike him to appease."[11]

Maxwell also makes the observation of my heart, "It would be so much easier if we could just be thankful, instead of faithful." It is interesting we often refer to an apparent *no* from God as an unanswered prayer. Do we think only God's immediate *yes!* is God truly being God? Mary and Martha may have been tempted to think the same. Jesus was answering definitively. His answer was simply, "This will end in the glory of God." Rather than a sign of an unloving God, this is a loving and high honor. This is the highest purpose for which any situation or circumstance can exist.

So if all of this is true, how are we to respond? How do we walk this narrow path? Even God must admit that although his voice leads us and the way is secure, we walk in a world of illusion, shadow, and fog. As Paul says, while we search for the true image of God, even on our best days, we look for reality through a dimly lit and smudged mirror.

Let me give you some practical encouragement. We will all be in the place of Mary, Martha, and Lazarus. The names and places will change, but the gravity of a sin-soaked world and limited perspective will feel just the same. Ask yourself, "Am I missing something here? Am I expecting God to act like I would act? Do I trust God more than I trust myself? Which end am I pushing toward?"

The loving thing about God is that when he waits, he gives us opportunity to trust him. If he answered when we asked every time, it wouldn't look like he was doing it. We would be doing it. Our timing would be paramount, and our desired reality would supersede the one that actually exists.

Have you ever heard someone say they don't think they need the gospel? *I don't need God. I work hard. I got the job. I get paid. I manage the money. I play by my rules and the sky isn't falling. If this is what I need saving from, just leave me where I am. I'm not drowning.*

Friend, the worst thing God could ever do to us is to never reveal himself to us—no Genesis 1–3, no Old Testament law, no Scripture, no Jesus, no revealed righteousness. We would be sheep without fences, guides, or guards. This sounds like freedom until the wolves come. In reality, this is anarchy. It is a world of danger. It is also our default desire. It would be tragically unloving to leave us in that state. However, until we see the wolves, we never appreciate the purpose of the guards. Until we find ourselves lost, we never appreciate the guides and fences. Until we are brought to that point, we won't think we need God.

The most loving thing a heavenly Father can do is to reveal that hopelessness to us. A loving God will continually show us we are not him. In love, God calls us through the painful, the dark, the shallow, and the unfulfilling to cultivate our joy and trust in him, not ourselves. In God's love, he will lead us to fall in love with his glory. Often we don't like this. When we hear "fall in love," all we hear is "fall."

Sadly our churches are full of people who love God (or the idea of God) but not his glory. These people are locked in an infinite loop of frustration. They love God in the cape, but they don't see God behind the glasses. They are confused, even angry when he doesn't act the way they want him to. However, when you love God's character, you love God's ways because they point to his character. His glory is shown even in the ways that bring lament, the ones that remind us that this is not home and that we waste away and are but dust, the ones that remind us we are headed toward a beautiful reality with God as displayed in Revelation 21. We aren't there yet. But in his grace and his timing, God is pulling us there.

Author and pastor Cole Feix talks about the pull and tension of God in these words:

> If you would just realize that that is the order of things, you could have life everlasting through (God). But you are too busy settling for the things you are trying to create on your own. And it is God's love that compels him to reveal to us that we cannot do it on our own. One of the primary ways God does that is by waiting. Waiting for his time, for his plan, for his grace.[12]

Belief is a question of trust. Do you trust God? Mary and Martha trusted God. They wanted to believe in God. We even find ourselves trusting God, wanting to believe in God. But we still have questions, and that's okay. The Bible is full of questions from people wanting to follow God, the patient, long-suffering, slow-to-anger God who hears them all. It's okay to let the question rattle in our hearts, "God, when are you going to make yourself mighty through good things?"

But the greatest answer is this: Trust God. Trust God to bring about his glory. Trust God that his glory is our greatest good. Trust God that his glory is the revelation of himself, and a good father will not keep himself hidden.

Do you trust God? His glory frees you from worldly standards. He has written your every day. His love compels him to reach out to us even in our rebellion. Are you willing to wait for the glory of God, knowing often the glory of God is revealed, even deepened, in the waiting? Isaiah 40:28–31 reminds us,

> Have you not known? Have you not heard? The LORD is the everlasting God, the Creator of the ends of the earth. He does not faint or grow weary; his understanding is unsearchable. He gives power to the faint, and to him who has no might he increases strength. Even youths shall faint and be weary, and young men shall fall exhausted; but they who wait for the LORD shall renew their strength; they shall mount up with wings like eagles; they shall run and not be weary; they shall walk and not faint.

Take time to respond to this. Actually respond. Pray your heart out to God in the situation you are in. Question, ask, and evaluate. But know God will receive the glory. There is no greater thing he could give. He is a good Father we can trust.

CHAPTER 4

The God Who Gives Doubt

Here is a difficult reality: Joel Osteen, John Piper, Westboro Baptist Church, Rob Bell, and many others all sit down with the same Bible, yet they think, lead, and teach very different messages about very different gods—all under the name of Jesus. Why is this? Sometimes we are more in tune with a god of our own cultural making or desire than we are with the God of the Bible.

The God of the Bible creates tension. He is messy. He says hard things. It is easier to run to an idea of God as a god who exists simply to make us happy or comfortable, one who lives to make us feel wanted, validated, and keep us safe. If God is light and life, then Christianity must be clear and free from doubt, right?

Doubt is a tricky thing in the Christian life. It breaks our "everything is good all the time" Christianity. It makes us actually wrestle with real fears. Doubt is a very big thing, a very weighty device.

I was reminded of this truth recently. I was sitting in my office when another member of our staff rushed up to my door and knocked. The person apologized for the interruption but said it was an emergency. One of our neighbors was on the line and needed to get a hold of me promptly. I picked up the phone with trepidation to find my neighbor filled with urgent angst.

Our neighbor has two dogs and a cat. She works during the day, and my wife, Allison, will often go over to her house to let the dogs out for a bit and make sure everything is generally okay. Our neighbor also has an alarm system like the Eye of Sauron. It sees all and knows all. There are cameras, sensors, a catapult, crocodile-laden moats, and that giant ball from Indiana Jones. It's all there.

The system also sends my neighbor an alert on her phone whenever a status changes—if a door or window is open, etc. She had received an alert that the back door was left open. She assumed after Allison had gone over to tend to the dogs that she had mistakenly left the door open. This set her in a panic because her cat is a runner. Moreover, behind their house and across a moderate fence, there lives a pit bull who *loves* cats.

I understood this panic and had great sympathy for my neighbor. I also grew up with a cat that was a runner. I spent many hours of my childhood walking through dark neighborhoods, lightly tapping a tuna can with a fork. When our neighbor was unable to get a hold of my wife, she called me and asked if I could run over to the house and check on the situation.

I got in my car, drove to her house, and went to the front door only to find it locked. I went around the back and tried to get a peak over the fence. I didn't see a cat or the remains of a cat. I also couldn't see the back door, so I decided to hop the fence to get a better look.

Vastly overestimating my ability to simply hop over a fence, I ended up getting my shoe stuck on the top of the fence while my other leg dangled just inches above the ground. People were driving by and looking inquisitively. I tried to wave and look friendly so they wouldn't call the cops.

Long story short (including a scratched-up pair of shoes), I was able to eventually get into the house. As I entered the house, I found two dogs yipping and jumping, excited I was there, and one cat standing in the corner, very emotionally disturbed and suspicious of my presence. I also found that the back door was locked and had apparently been locked the entire time. It was a false alarm.

I called my neighbor and told her everything was fine (except my pride and reputation in the neighborhood). She sighed deeply and repeated over and over, "Thank you! Thank you!" She had been really upset. Why? Because she felt something we all feel from time to time. She had a fear of the unknown.

This is a silly story. It is funny because it's relatable. We are all finite, limited creatures. Our perceptions of the unknown, our guesses and assumptions about the future (i.e., what might be) inform and push on how we act in the present. They greatly influence what we do and don't do. Much of our life is dictated by the perceived avoidance of unwanted situations to come. We are constantly preparing for certain outcomes that may or may not ever be. We have doubts and fears because we don't have knowledge.

When we think of God, we don't assume God is a god who gives doubt. That would be mean. God is not a god of confusion. He knows the future, knows his plans, carries us, and never leaves or forsakes us. And by all means, we can't doubt a circumstance because then we don't have faith, and we wouldn't be believing

God is good. After all, Jesus is the Light. He wouldn't want us to be in the dark. He would never give us doubt, uncertainty, and questions. Right?

"Then after this he said to the disciples, 'Let us go to Judea again.' The disciples said to him, 'Rabbi, the Jews were just now seeking to stone you, and are you going there again?'" (John 11:7–16).

This is a very pointed statement from Jesus. It is also a very loaded question from the disciples. To go back to Judea at that time seemed to them the surest way to commit suicide.

Let's do a quick flashback to John 10. Jesus is with his disciples in Jerusalem. The Jewish leaders are questioning him, saying, "Tell us. Are you the Christ?" Jesus says, "I told you, and you do not believe." Despite all the signs that pointed to Jesus and the truths he taught, they still did not believe because, as Jesus says, they were not of his sheep. If they were, they would know, as Jesus said, "I and the Father are one" (John 10:30). Then they picked up rocks to stone him for blasphemy. He, being a man, was claiming also to be God.

They try to stone Jesus and arrest him. He escapes and goes across the Jordan River. He is safe ... for now. But things are still heated. So when the disciples hear Jesus say they are to go back to this region of Judea, they are on alert. Why would Jesus put a fruitful ministry in jeopardy for a life-threatening trip to Judea? After all, they know the situation doesn't warrant his immediate attention. They know he can raise someone from the dead if need be. Plus, he said this wasn't going to end in death. Jesus had even healed a boy before who was more than twenty miles away. He is the master over distance. The disciples know—they believe—that a simple snap of his fingers could solve the problem. Given the realities the disciples knew, it would be lunacy for Jesus to go back. There is much danger.

So after this, Jesus says, "Let us go to Judea again." Jesus is challenging the disciples, and the disciples are challenging him to a battle of who knows best. Jesus is in extreme danger. The disciples are saying, "Don't you realize?"

Jesus knows he is in extreme danger, but he also knows he is *not* in extreme danger. He is not worried. He is neither hesitant nor flustered. He is not pressed to go. He simply says now is the time. This is the time Jesus chooses to go where he chooses into what he chooses.

He goes on to explain, "Are there not twelve hours in the day? If anyone walks in the day, he does not stumble, because he sees the light of this world. But if anyone walks in the night, he stumbles, because the light is not in him" (John 11:9–10).

We can be honest. This is weird. This is one of those sensei moments when Jesus says some words that seemingly carry no meaning and waves his hand, and then everyone's heads nod in reluctant yet self-preserving agreement. *Of course, Jesus. I was just about to say that ... about the light and the hours. I'm totally tracking with you.*

But let's call a spade a spade. This is confusing. What Jesus says on the surface is that there are twelve hours in a day to get things done. At this time in history, when the sun went down, you didn't simply turn on floodlights. When the light went away, you were done. There are twelve hours of light and twelve hours of darkness. Therefore, the day has both opportunity and limitation. There is a time to do work when you can because a time comes when you can't.

What Jesus is saying on a deeper level is that the path to the cross was well lit for him. All the grief, the questions, the danger, the pain—it was the lit path. He is not being flippant about this. This is not a "ye of little faith" accusation. It is a statement of fact. Jesus says he is here to do a job. He has a time frame to do that—a twelve-hour day. Neither the disciples' concern nor a different strategy could lengthen that time. The religious leaders' hostility could not shorten it. It is what it is.

Jesus says this is the appointed time for him. While he walks in this well-lit path, he knows he will not stumble, because this is the will of God. This is the revelation of the glory of God.

This is extremely important for us. We can be honest and admit that from our perspective, it is sometimes difficult to keep believing in the goodness of God. From the ground level, it can appear to us that even though we are God's children—he loves us, and we love him—sometimes it seems he does not care about us anymore.

It is okay to admit. The psalms are littered with that lament. When Jesus was going to the cross, many people were questioning God's goodness on his behalf. *If he is truly loved by God, won't God step in at some point to stop this? How long can this go on before Jesus displays his power? If Jesus is Lord and he is in charge, is this the path he has for me as well?*

But Jesus's words are important. He says this is the path. This is the way. This is well lit for him. When we walk in the well-lit path of God, there is no true threat, for all things are working together for good. Are there still obstacles? Certainly. Is there still pain? Absolutely. Understand there are still obstacles when you walk in the light of the Spirit of God with the Word of God as a guide.

There do seem to be obstacles for us, but they merely *seem* to be obstacles because we expect God to give us a path without obstacles. Therefore, we see them as hindrances to the path. To God, obstacles are simply part of the path itself. Sometimes the greatest obstacle in our path is the misguided notion that we will have a path without obstacles. This is pride. It is one of the ways we are lied to and deceived.

Walking in the light does not mean walking easily, but it means walking with an understanding that *whom* God knows, he leads into *what* he knows, and he is with us through it all. Cancer, loss, unmet expectations, broken relationships—these things are a part of life. One walks through them in the light of the day, understanding them as opportunities to see God glorified. Another walks through them in the darkness of night, seeing them as stumbling blocks. They suppose them to be merely reasons or opportunities to reject or sin against God.

Believers will always encounter opposition. But the tough stuff, the catalysts to questions, the things that burn down the straw man of our humanism, they don't break our salvation or confidence in God. They actually make it sure. They strengthen it. By God's grace they strengthen us. They actually give us joy. They cause us to worship.

These are not just things that happen *to* us. There are real obstacles to the Christian walk and walking in light of the gospel. Being a Christian costs something now. It will cost more in the future. Saying that you believe the Bible is the inerrant Word of God, that it is true about who we are and who God is, and that you submit to it above all else used to get you applause in some circles. Now it is more likely to isolate you. In some places it will get you killed.

Christians, some of us will lose our jobs for the sake of the gospel. Some of us will be bypassed for opportunity. We will lose relationships and much, much more. I shudder to think about what our children will face in opposition to the gospel of Jesus Christ. It has happened before. It is happening at an even greater depth and speed now. It is coming for us. I'm sure you are glad you are reading this life-affirming book!

This is the "bad news" for the Christian. But here is the great news. Consider the words of David, a man who knew well what following God could cost. He writes in Psalm 23:1–4,

> The LORD is my shepherd, I shall not want. He makes me lie down in green pastures. He leads me beside still waters. He restores my soul. He leads me in paths of righteousness for his name's sake. Even though I walk through the valley of the shadow of death, I will fear no evil, for you are with me.

Don't let the familiarity of those verses keep you from understanding their gravity. Sometimes the well-worn paths are well-worn for a reason. Read the words again. For those of us in Christ, we will not want. We will have green pastures and still waters because our God is good and sustains us.

But don't miss this. The paths of righteousness often lead through the valley of the shadow of death. However, this is the hope of martyrs. You can do whatever you want to us. Take whatever you like. The valley of the shadow of death is not dark for us. It is lit. It is part of our twelve-hour day. It is the work appointed for us. This valley is green, and these waters are still because God has led us here. Why? He has led us here for his name's sake. God will receive the glory. Look at John 11:4, which says, "This illness does not lead to death. It is for the glory of God." How much we esteem the glory of God will greatly affect how much we appreciate the path he leads us on to receive it.

The path to the cross was well lit for Jesus. Was he physically in danger? Yes. But the glory of God was never in danger. This is the path. It will lead to God's glory. God's glory is best. It is preeminent. It is the highest aim for us, our greatest joy. It is our purpose and our design. Without it, we are broken. When we seek God's glory above all, there is no danger. God's glory wins.

Friend, the path to wherever God is taking you, though it seems temporarily dark, is eternally well lit for those in Christ Jesus. The gospel gives us this perspective. "Though the fig tree should not blossom, nor the fruit be on the vines, the produce of the olive fail and the fields yield no food, the flock be cut off from the fold and there be no herd in the stalls, yet I will rejoice in the LORD; I will take joy in the God of my salvation" (Habakkuk 3:17–18).

What makes you glad? You might identify several things, depending on your definition of the word *glad*. As I am writing this, I am sitting in the corner of a local coffee shop only a few miles from the base of the Rocky Mountains in Colorado. It is cold, rainy, and foggy, and the coffee has just enough caffeine to keep me cognizant amidst the comfort. I'm in my own element.

I'm wearing big headphones piping music into my brain, the soundtrack to my introverted haven.

This makes me glad. Depending on your wiring, you might have different things from which you derive gladness. Maybe it's a beach. Perhaps it is a person or group of people. Perhaps it's a movie, a memory, a book, a favorite dish, or a surprise. Regardless, the way we derive gladness says a lot about us. It helps us define what we value, where we find rest, and what we anticipate.

"After saying these things, he said to them, 'Our friend Lazarus has fallen asleep, but I go to awaken him.' The disciples said to him, 'Lord, if he has fallen asleep, he will recover.' Now Jesus had spoken of his death, but they thought that he meant taking rest in sleep" (John 11:11–13).

John Calvin, the reformer, in response to this passage notes, "Christ was remarkably kind in putting up with such stupidity from the disciples."[13] I don't know if I would go as far as Calvin, but he makes some good points (wink). There are things about Jesus that made the disciples glad. They loved the miracles. They loved the crowds. They were the entourage of the hottest man in show business.

Being a disciple of Jesus had a lot of benefits—adventure, intrigue, and wisdom at every turn. You never knew what would happen next, but whatever it was, it would be amazing. But the disciples were a lot like us. What made them glad was usually what made them comfortable. The joy of the Lord was Jesus's strength, but it was not quite yet theirs.

When Jesus said Lazarus had fallen asleep, it gave the disciples a glimmer of hope. He is asleep. He is resting. This is good news.

But they're really thinking about how Jesus doesn't have to go back into danger now. Even more importantly, they assume they don't have to follow him into danger. Everything is fine. Then Jesus makes it messy. "Then Jesus told them plainly, 'Lazarus has died, and for your sake I am glad that I was not there, so that you may believe. But let us go to him'" (John 11:14–15).

Gulp.

Remember John's purpose statement. His goal is belief. Belief for the reader that Jesus is the Christ, the Son of God, and that by believing, they might have life in his name. Jesus says plainly, "Lazarus has died, and for your sake I am *glad* I was not there."

Glad. This makes Jesus glad? Does it bother you how unapologetic, how cavalier Jesus seems about this? Remember where he is going. He is going to the cross. He is going to be abandoned by these very same disciples. He is going to cause mass confusion among his loved ones. Jesus is walking into excruciating physical and emotional trauma that ultimately ends in his own death. Jesus is going to die, and it is making him … glad?

Jesus is glad not because this is going to be fun. He is not glad because Lazarus is dead but because something bigger is at stake here. What is at stake is the belief of the disciples. "For *your* sake I am glad that I was not there, so that *you* may believe."

The disciples will need this belief. Up to this point, they believed in a God who could raise the dead. He has done that before. He didn't need to prove to them that he had power over death. They believe in a God who can raise the dead. But they don't believe in a God who dies. They don't believe in a God who waits. They don't believe in a God who loses. They don't believe in a God who causes _____ or walks into

_____.

This is important for us, especially in times of spiritual, physical, or emotional suffering. We need this when our bright, shiny image of God gets very cloudy. There are two things we need to know about God's attitude toward us and our situation in these times. One we will discuss later. The other is something easy to read but hard to apply. It is about Jesus's perspective.

John tells us something about Jesus, and we can rest secure on this. For those going through or toward trial, into what doesn't make sense, toward biblical truth about God coming through difficulty all for the sake of the gospel and the glory of God, what is Jesus's attitude toward you? John shows us Jesus's attitude toward you is not abandonment. It is not testing or anger. Jesus is *glad* for you. He is glad because you have an opportunity to believe through this and trust God as never before. That makes Jesus glad.

Jesus is glad for us just like he is here with the disciples. He tells them they are going to learn a very deep truth. It is a truth they are going to question, a truth they will need, and a truth they will love. What is this truth? Jesus is God, and he is in control. Friend, Jesus is God, and he is in control. *But it doesn't look like— Why did he have to— I never saw this coming—*Jesus is God, and he is in control.

The disciples are going to be right there in a week. They are going to be raising those very same objections. *How could you let them take you, Jesus? How could you let them say those things about you, Jesus? How could you let them cause such pain to you, Jesus? Why aren't you stepping in, Jesus? How could you let them crucify you, Jesus?*

How could you die, Jesus? How could you let them take you down, wrap you up, and put you in a tomb, Jesus? How could you let us wait, Jesus? Are you really who you said you are, Jesus?

They will need this faith. We will need this faith. This is big for the disciples. Jesus is glad for them so that they may believe.

So how are they to respond? How are we to respond when we face these questions and situations? "So Thomas, called the Twin, said to his fellow disciples, 'Let us also go, that we may die with him'" (John 11:16).

I'm going to stick up for somebody here. This may not be popular, but I think it is right. We have totally Eeyored one of Jesus's disciples, and I think it is undue.

Do you remember Eeyore, Winnie the Pooh's gloomy little donkey friend? In order to accurately assess Eeyore and his melancholy worldview, let's take a look at a few of my favorite Eeyore quotes.

"When someone says, 'How do you do,' just say that you didn't."[14] "When stuck in the river, it is best to dive and swim to the bank yourself before someone drops a large stone on your chest in an attempt to hoosh you there."[15]

This quote recalls a conversation between Eeyore and one of his friends:

> "It's snowing still," said Eeyore gloomily.
> "So it is."
> "And freezing."
> "Is it?"
> "Yes," said Eeyore, "However," he said, brightening up a little, "We haven't had an earthquake lately."[16]

Eeyore's countenance is perhaps best displayed in this summary:

The old grey donkey, Eeyore, stood by himself in a thistly corner of the forest, his front feet well apart, his head on one side, and thought about things. Sometimes he thought sadly to himself, "Why?" and sometimes he thought, "Wherefore?" and sometimes he thought, "Inasmuch as which?" and sometimes he didn't quite know what he was thinking about.[17]

This is the picture much of Christianity has painted of Thomas the disciple. Poor Thomas, doubting Thomas.

But what if Thomas is given to us not as a slapstick sidekick picture of doubt but as a picture of something much more?

Thomas's name is mentioned eleven times in the Bible. It occurs only one time each in Matthew, Mark, Luke, and Acts, and even then it is only in a list of the disciples. There is nothing else remarkable mentioned about him. Nothing is noteworthy. John mentions Thomas's name seven times. The first mention is here in chapter 11.

"Let us also go, that we may die with him" he says. How do we assume he says this? If it were Peter, we would read it as a call to action, the revealing of yet another reactionary moment of initiative. If it were someone less volatile, we might read it more matter-of-factly, a leader's levelheaded assessment of the disciples' needed action. Because it is Thomas and we know him as "doubting Thomas," we assume he says it with a tone of defeated sarcasm. But does the text say that? What did the other disciples say? Either we don't know, or they said nothing at all.

Either way, John makes a point to show us something about Thomas here. Perhaps John purposely introduces Thomas's actions as an example of *how* to believe Jesus is the Christ, the Son of God, and by believing have life in his name, especially in times of doubt.

So how are we to look at Thomas? Frederick Bruner notes, "However Thomas felt or spoke, he does at least want to accompany Jesus."[18] John MacArthur, a man with his own reputation of having a bit of cynicism, states, "Thomas negatively led him to believe he would die if they went to Jerusalem. On the other hand, his love for Jesus was so strong that he was willing to die with Him."[19] I like how William Barclay explains, "In his heart ... there was not expectant faith, but loyal despair. But upon one thing Thomas was determined—come what may, he would not quit."[20]

Barclay illustrates the fortitude of Thomas in a compelling story told by writer Gilbert Frankau. Frankau shares the story of an officer friend of his in World War I. Frankau's friend was an artillery observation officer. His duty was to go up in a type of hot-air balloon held to the ground by a rope. From his unique perspective in the balloon, he would indicate to the gunners whether their shots were falling short of or going over the target.

Needless to say, this was a very precarious situation. Balloons are easy to see. They are slow. They do not make for a hasty getaway in the face of sudden threat. The men in these balloons became sitting targets for the guns and planes of the enemy.

Frankau said of his friend, "Every time he went up in that balloon, he was sick with nerves, but he would not quit." Barclay in his commentary expounds:

> This is the highest form of courage. It does not mean not being afraid. If we are not afraid it is the easier thing in the world to do a thing. Real courage means being perfectly aware of the worst that can happen, being sickeningly afraid of it, and yet doing the right thing. That was what Thomas was like that day. No man need ever be ashamed of being afraid; but he may well be ashamed of allowing his fear to stop him doing what in his heart of hearts he knows he ought to do.[21]

No matter how Thomas felt about the situation, he knew what had to be done. Whether he said it like Eeyore or William Wallace in *Braveheart* doesn't matter. Come what may, he is going with Jesus. Why would he do this? Because where Jesus is and where he is going, there is light.

Does Thomas have doubt? Yes. So do the rest of the disciples. So do Mary, Martha, and Lazarus. But lest we become distracted by the doubt of Thomas and the disciples themselves, let us consider God's purpose in creating the doubt. God sows doubt in Thomas and the disciples to reap faith. He plants seeds of doubt to rejoice as the faith grows. "Faith is the assurance of things hoped for, and the conviction of things not seen" (Hebrews 11:1).

We want faith. We need faith. Sometimes the most loving, strong, and indelible way God can give us faith is through doubt.

Though I walk through the valley of the shadow of death, I will fear no evil, for you are with me. Where God is, there is light.

Take comfort in this. Some people have that amazing, vibrant, take-on-the-world attitude in seasons of doubt. Trials are sources of joy for them. They have that kind of faith. Whether that is you or you're the type to say, "Let's go die with him," Jesus is glad because he is giving you faith.

Jesus says, "Let's go back to Judea." Let's go back to danger, back to what doesn't make sense, back on the road to the cross. Jesus has a job to do, a time to do it in, and while they won't see it now, he is so glad for their sake. He is glad that through this, they may believe Jesus is the Christ, the Son of God, and by believing, they may have life in his name.

Friend, what do you need to have a very honest discussion with God about? Where is he going that makes you uncomfortable? What is he doing that is forcing you to a perspective beyond yourself and your strength? Where is God pursuing you?

You say to yourself, *God, I'm staring at* _____. *It is dangerous and scary. But I know you are in this. I will go there with you and die with you.*

God I am staring at _____. *I want to believe! Help my heart believe!* _____ *has knocked me down. I'm not even close to the right path. I don't even know where to find you to know where or how to follow you. But I want to. Whatever it takes, I want to.*

"For your sake I am glad I was not there so that you may believe. But let us go to him" (John 11:15).

CHAPTER 5

The God Who Loses

They say you should never talk about religion or politics. So in this book about God, let's talk about politics. Let's assume you are a political right-wing conservative. What is your immediate reaction when a liberal, pro-abortion, marriage-redefining candidate is elected? What is your immediate reaction when your state capitol building has to take down a plaque containing the Ten Commandments or face the prospect of a sculpture being erected on the premises created by and promoting the church of Satan—all in the name of religious tolerance (a reality in my home state)?

Let's go a bit closer to home. What is your immediate reaction when someone you love is rejecting Christ or when someone ungodly succeeds? What about when you read the Bible and nothing happens? What is your response when you feel stuck in a situation you know God doesn't want you to get out of but just doesn't seem to be going anywhere?

What is your immediate reaction to loss or to hard news? How do you feel when this world basks in the glow of new levels of depravity and calls it *progress*? If God is so jealous for his name and his glory, why are there so many people freely trampling on his name for the sake of their own glory? We know in the end God will win the war. But right now, is God losing?

Let's remember where we are in our text. Jesus has stacked the deck against himself. He is walking into hostile territory that poses physical danger, but he is also inviting very real, deep questions, doubts, and accusations from people he loves. However, Jesus does so with a purpose. He is redefining for us the definitions of God's love, glory, and sovereignty. What is coming next is vitally important yet requires a word of caution. Before we proceed, let us establish the context for the discussion we are about to have and the environment in which it will take place.

I really like summer, not because I enjoy the blazing heat or poolside barbeques (which I do) but mainly because of two words: summer blockbusters. Summer is when Hollywood unloads the big guns. Each week there is a bevy of must-see films clawing for our time and attention and seeking to justify the otherwise awkward experience of sitting in a dark room with strangers eating Junior Mints.

A lot of movies recently have been adaptations of popular books. You may be someone who prefers the written story more than the film version. Perhaps you prefer the movie over the book version. If so, I apologize because I sincerely doubt this book will ever be made into a movie. You will have to read it. Just for the record, I would be played by a strong-jawed Ryan Gosling, and Michael Bay's adaptation would include massive explosions and gratuitous citywide architectural carnage. But I digress.

Both movie and book versions of stories have positives and negatives. For example, one of my favorite books is Orson Scott

Card's *Ender's Game.* I love reading it. The depth of characters, the articulate descriptions, the battles, and the symmetry of words—it is a fantastic work. Above that, the gravity of the book is found in its nuances of moral and ethical conflict. It challenges the reader to confront deeply presumed statutes of right, wrong, and situational ethic.

When I heard they were making the book into a movie, I was excited. My parents, who had not read the book, saw the movie and gave it a glowing review.

I bought my Junior Mints. I smooshed into my seat amongst rows of mouth-breathers stuffing their faces with popcorn. I saw it. I hated it.

Granted, they got all the action right, but the deeper emotions, the inner struggle and turmoil over moral ethics, and the very definitions of personhood were totally left out. I suppose you can only fit so much into a two-hour movie. Moreover, elongated scenes where the actors discuss moral ethos may not make for riveting on-screen drama (insert Michael Bay explosion). In my view the movie simply could not hold all of what was accomplished in the book.

By the same token (or Tolkien), consider the *Lord of the Rings* trilogy. I first tried to read *The Fellowship of the Ring* in my early teenage years. For those of us who are only familiar with reading on something that has to be intermittently plugged in, there used to be things called libraries. In these libraries there were things called books. You had to physically take a book to a person and check it out. If you went to the library and the book was unavailable, you had to ... wait. I know you must be wondering which of our dinosaurs we rode to these libraries.

It was on one such expedition that I went to the library and found *The Fellowship of the Ring*. It was absolutely massive. I was lost the whole time. I understood there was a ring, but not much else. In fact, there was one character I thought was three different characters the entire time. I finally got to the end of the book and realized there were still two more of these riddling behemoths. No thank you.

I cast aside the *Lord of the Rings* until many years later when Peter Jackson created his movie adaptations. As I watched the movies, suddenly so much more of the story became clear. I was able to keep the characters straight. I could visualize the places and what made them distinct. The visual helped me understand the greater story and not get bogged down in the particular words or descriptions.

Here's where I'm going with this. For those of you who love the nuances, the ethical and moral struggles, and the behind-the-scenes insights, John is not giving that to us in these verses. For those who love the action, bullet points, easy-to-understand linear accounts, John has written this way.

In this chapter I want us to explore a weighty bit of text—one that could be expounded upon in libraries and volumes of books. There is a lot here. But I want us to touch on the high points. I want us to focus on the intent of our discussion and most importantly, the intent of John in writing this portion of Scripture. We are not going to be able to take apart every little piece and examine it.

Before we start, I want to skip to the end and tell you what we are going to find. In looking at the next few verses, we are going to have more questions than answers. This is appropriate.

This is good. Why is it good that we end up with more questions than answers here? Because that is the way the Spirit inspired John to write this. It may be messier, but it is best.

> Now when Jesus came, he found that Lazarus had already been in the tomb four days. Bethany was near Jerusalem, about two miles off, and many of the Jews had come to Martha and Mary to console them concerning their brother.
>
> So when Martha heard that Jesus was coming, she went and met him, but Mary remained seated in the house.
>
> Martha said to Jesus, "Lord, if you had been here, my brother would not have died. But even now I know that whatever you ask from God, God will give you."
>
> Jesus said to her, "Your brother will rise again." Martha said to him, "I know that he will rise again in the resurrection on the last day."
>
> Jesus said to her, "I am the resurrection and the life. Whoever believes in me, though he die, yet shall he live, and everyone who lives and believes in me shall never die. Do you believe this?"
>
> She said to him, "Yes, Lord; I believe that you are the Christ, the Son of God, who is coming into the world."
>
> When she had said this, she went and called her sister Mary, saying in private, "The Teacher is here and is calling for you." And when she heard it, she rose quickly and went to him.

Now Jesus had not yet come into the village, but was still in the place where Martha had met him. When the Jews who were with her in the house, consoling her, saw Mary rise quickly and go out, they followed her, supposing that she was going to the tomb to weep there.

Now when Mary came to where Jesus was and saw him, she fell at his feet, saying to him, "Lord, if you had been here, my brother would not have died."

When Jesus saw her weeping, and the Jews who had come with her also weeping, he was deeply moved in his spirit and greatly troubled. And he said, "Where have you laid him?" They said to him, "Lord, come and see."

Jesus wept. So the Jews said, "See how he loved him!"

But some of them said, "Could not he who opened the eyes of the blind man also have kept this man from dying?" (John 11:17–37)

I've titled this chapter "The God Who Loses." This is risky. It is important to note Jesus did not *lose* in the sense that he was caught off guard or was defeated in a battle of strength. Perhaps a more appropriate word would be Jesus *conceded*. This was the plan all along.

However, to those present, by all accounts it looked like Jesus had lost. Jesus let it appear that way. First of all, John notes Lazarus has been in the tomb four days. This is important because at this time there was a rabbinic tradition amongst the Jews. They believed that after someone died, the person's soul stuck around for three days. It did so in the hopes that the body would come back to life or resuscitate. However, after three days the soul left, never to return. It was finished. There was no hope for the person. If there was any hope that Jesus might swoop in at the last second to save the day, it is out the window. At day four Jesus has lost that opportunity.

Secondly John notes Bethany was only two miles from Jerusalem. Jesus is very near in proximity to an area in which he is not wanted by many. This puts him in extreme physical danger. Remember, just a few days ago, people tried to arrest and kill him in Jerusalem. Jesus is very near those who want him dead.

Thirdly John tells us that many Jews had come to the house. This means many things, but if nothing else, it means there is an audience for this—not just any audience but an audience who saw or participated in the religious leaders wanting him stoned. This is the audience containing those who in a week would be raising palm branches and shouting, "Hosanna!" This audience also includes those who shortly thereafter would be raising their fists and shouting, "Crucify him!" It likely included those who would do both.

Either way, Jesus is walking into a very difficult situation. Mary and Martha had gone all in on Jesus. His actions are confusing. The situation is embarrassing for Mary and Martha, and it is played out in front of a crowd. Everyone involved will have an accusation, an assumption, and an admission.

Let's begin with Martha. We are perhaps familiar with her from the story in Luke 10. Martha is busy serving. Mary is sitting at Jesus's feet. Martha wants Jesus to instruct Mary to get up and start helping her. Jesus informs Martha that Mary has chosen what is best by simply sitting at Jesus's feet at this time, not letting busyness become a distraction. This is the same house, the same Mary, and the same Martha.

Martha is the first to go out and meet Jesus. She meets him immediately with the words, "Lord, if you had been here, my brother would not have died." At its basest level, what is Martha's accusation? *Jesus, you lost. We knew you loved Lazarus. We knew you could heal. We knew you could come. Every hope we propped up all came crashing down when you didn't come. Jesus, you lost.*

Given her dire accusation, Martha still has a hopeful assumption. "But even now I know that whatever you ask from God, God will give you." Jesus said to her, "Your brother will rise again." Martha said to him, "I know that he will rise again in the resurrection on the last day" (John 11:22–24).

Her assumption? *Jesus, you are still able.* Note that Martha does not believe he *will* raise Lazarus from the dead. From her objection in verse 39, we know she doesn't think that is on the table. To Martha, it is simple. *Jesus, thousands of years of history and faithful witness in the lives of others as well as everything you've said and done didn't go out the window when you seemingly didn't come through for me.*

We see this confidence in two main ways. First she calls him *Lord*. She doesn't just call him *Jesus* or *friend*, citing the personal relationship and trying to make Jesus feel guilty. She calls him *Lord*. Despite the whirlwind and circumstance, she tethers her anchor to Jesus as Lord.

Second, we see this confidence displayed in that she still hopes for Jesus's resurrection. She knows Lazarus will rise on the last day. She believes in a God who will resurrect—who will have final victory over death. While she knows he lost this battle, he is still able to win the war.

This leads Martha to her ultimate admission. *Jesus, I still believe.* We are going to sink our teeth into what Jesus says in verses 25 and 26 later, so stay tuned. But for our purposes now, let's look briefly at his words. "I am the resurrection and the life. Whoever believes in me, though he die, yet shall he live, and everyone who lives and believes in me shall never die. Do you believe this?"

In other words, Jesus is asking Martha if she believes beyond what she knows she believes. Is her horizon of belief beyond where her feet stand in the here and now?

Again, recall John's purpose in writing this—so that we might believe Jesus is the Christ, the Son of God, and that by believing, we may have life in his name. This is the point, the crux, and the question of the book of John: "Do you believe this?"

She says, "Yes, Lord, I believe that you are the Christ, the Son of God, who is coming into the world."

Martha's accusation: *Jesus, you lost.*

Her assumption: *Jesus, you are still able.*

Her admission: *I still believe in you.*

Would that be your reaction in Martha's situation?

Because we have taken a look at Martha, let's turn to her sister, Mary. John describes her encounter with Jesus.

> When she had said this, she went and called her sister Mary, saying in private, "The Teacher is here and is calling for you."

And when she heard it, she rose quickly and went to him.

Now Jesus had not yet come into the village, but was still in the place where Martha had met him.

When the Jews who were with her in the house, consoling her, saw Mary rise quickly and go out, they followed her, supposing that she was going to the tomb to weep there.

Now when Mary came to where Jesus was and saw him, she fell at his feet, saying to him, "Lord, if you had been here, my brother would not have died." (John 11:28–32)

Remember how we said we would have more questions than answers as we walk through the actions of this passage? Mary's actions with Jesus lead us to a few questions. Why didn't Mary go with Martha the first time? Well, we don't know. Maybe she did not want to alert the Jerusalem Jews of Jesus's presence. Maybe she simply didn't know Jesus was coming. The word may have only been given to Martha initially. Perhaps Mary did not want to offend the large group of mourners who had gathered to support the family. If she and Martha both left, who would be there to tend to the guests?

These are all noble reasons. But perhaps her reasoning was due to a deeper hurt. Maybe she was simply too upset to talk with Jesus right then. Perhaps she did not know what to say to him, or worse, perhaps she was afraid of saying what she wanted to say to him. Regardless, John tells us at this time she gets up and goes. She meets Jesus with an accusation.

What is Mary's accusation? *Jesus, you lost.* She gives the same words as her sister, Martha. "Lord, if you had been here, my brother would not have died."

How many times do you think they had said this around the house? *If Jesus comes, then our brother will not die. If Jesus comes, then our brother will not die. If Jesus comes, then our brother will not die.*

It was not as if, upon Martha's return, Mary asked her, "What did you say? Oh, that's good. I'll get him with that!" Rather she gives an open, honest accusation. She says exactly what she is feeling. She says what she is thinking. *Jesus, you lost.*

Notice Jesus doesn't rebuke Mary or Martha. Strangely that is what we somewhat expect. But this situation is not as similar to our account in Luke 10, where one of the sisters is in the right and one in the wrong. Jesus understands their perspective. He understands their pain. He absorbs their accusation as only God can.

Like Martha, what we see of Mary does not end with her assumption. She still has an admission. Her admission is this: *I want to believe.* Martha declares unshaking confidence in Jesus's ability. Mary throws herself at Jesus's feet. She is not pointing her finger at Jesus's chest. She is not holding her hands on her hips, waiting for tardy Jesus to justify himself and apologize. Rather she throws her whole body down at Jesus's feet in humble submission. In confusion, she says, "Jesus, you are still God. You are still Lord. But Jesus, I don't get it."

Have you ever been there?

When I turned sixteen, my dad sat me down to have a real man-to-man conversation. I had the wide-eyed enthusiasm of an invincible boy ready to take on the world in a two-thousand-pound speed machine. I had a new driver's license. I had new freedom. My curfew was pushed back a bit. I thought I was a big deal.

My dad sat me down and said, "Ryan, trust is given, and trust is earned. I give you my trust as my son, but you have to earn my trust through your actions."

That is wisdom.

Here, Mary says, "Jesus, trust is given, and trust is earned. You still hold my trust as my Lord. I fall down at your feet. I plead to you. But my trust account in you has been wiped clean by this action. Jesus, I love you. You are Lord. You are God. I am not. But right now I am going to need you to carry my belief." Much like the desperate father of the sick boy in Mark 9, she cries, "*I believe! Help my unbelief!*"

Mary's accusation: *Jesus, you lost.*

Mary's assumption: *You are still God.*

Mary's admission: *I want to believe.*

Is that how you would have responded in Mary's situation?

While Mary and Martha receive most of the camera time, there is a peripheral group playing a major role, specifically the mourners. They also have an accusation, an assumption, and an admission. To understand the perspective of the mourners, we must first understand something about them.

At this time in the first century, it was rude if someone was mourning and you did not go along. In modern times we may pull our car over for a funeral procession as a sign of respect and camaraderie. They would have joined the procession whether they knew the deceased or not. They were simply mourning death.

There were even professional mourners. It was thought at that time the louder the wailing in the wake of one's passing, the more honor it brought to the deceased. There were actually people who were paid to weep and wail, to scream and moan. It was a means of honor. It was just what they did.

So when we lump a group together as "the mourners," we must consider who these individuals are. Some are friends. Some are family. Some are merely curious, and others are people along the route. Certainly some are intrigued by the whole Jesus dynamic, wondering what will happen next. Some simply don't knowing what to expect.

> When Jesus saw her weeping, and the Jews who had come with her also weeping, he was deeply moved in his spirit and greatly troubled.
>
> And he said, "Where have you laid him?" They said to him, "Lord, come and see."
>
> Jesus wept.
>
> So the Jews said, "See how he loved him!"
>
> But some of them said, "Could not he who opened the eyes of the blind man also have kept this man from dying?" (John 11:33–37)

The mourners' accusation: *Jesus, you lost.* They may have simply thought Jesus loved Lazarus and now is in mourning over his death. Some may have known what Jesus could have done and are now simply disappointed—one more "messiah" falling short. He gave it the old college try, but in the end he couldn't do it—or so they assume. Whether they know what Jesus could have done or not, they know he didn't do it.

They think this is an embarrassment for Jesus.

Their accusation gives way to an assumption. *You are in question.* This event (or lack thereof) raises questions about Jesus. If he could, why didn't he? If he didn't, is it because he couldn't? If this man claims to be God, either he is a God who lost or a God who couldn't win or something else altogether. Either way, this man is in question.

The swarm of questions leads to an admission from the mourners. *Jesus, we doubt.* They are not doubting that he loved Lazarus or loves Martha and Mary. They sympathize with him. They are prepared to mourn with him. No matter their background, what they know of Christ, or what they have seen of Jesus, their impression of Jesus now is doubt.

Sure, he loved him, but if these stories about the blind guy being healed are true, couldn't he have kept this man from dying? This debacle is causing them to doubt not just his divinity or power but also everything they have heard about him and everything they've seen. For them, Jesus's signs may have pointed to a greater power, but now they have seen the limit of that power.

Jesus is God? They have doubt.

The mourners' accusation: *Jesus, you lost.*

The mourners' assumption: *You are in question.*

The mourners' admission: *We doubt.*

Is that how you would have responded?

On May 17, 2006, David Blaine was plunged into dangerous water. The well-known magician, illusionist, and artist was planning yet another crowd-stirring endurance stunt in which he was submerged in an eight-foot, water-filled globe. This was done in front of Lincoln Center in New York City. The plan was that for seven days and seven nights, using tubes for air and nutrition, Blaine's body would be publicly tested against the eroding and degrading effects of water without oxygen.

The New York Times' Kenneth Silverman wrote, "His feat of endurance brought a diverse crowd of thousands of New Yorkers together, renewing for a while the city's waning spirit of community."[22]

Not only did Blain stay in the water, but for his grand finale, he would attempt to hold his breath underwater to defeat the current world record of eight minutes and fifty-eight seconds.

The crowd watched intently. The camera lenses zoomed as the seconds passed on the clock. Around the seven-minute mark, Blaine began to show signs of concern. Support divers made the difficult call to pull Blaine up and out of the water after a completed seven minutes and twelve seconds—one minute and fifty seconds short of his goal.

Blaine had lost. As the bystanders gave polite applause at such a great attempted feat, *The Washington Post* stated, "Blaine represented an opportunity to see something unbelievable."[23]

To many people, Jesus was like David Blaine. He did some really neat, inexplicable stuff. He attracted crowds who marveled. He did a lot of great things around real people in real situations. But at the end of the day, a lot of people simply think he was a guy who did some miracles and taught good morals and love, but there was not much else to him.

For Martha, Mary, and the mourners, they may have echoed *The Washington Post* quip, "Jesus represented an opportunity to see something unbelievable."

We have been in these situations. We prayed and prayed for healing, and none came. We prayed and prayed for justice, but the unjust got away. We prayed and prayed for righteousness, but greed, licentiousness, and humanistic revelry won the day.

In times like these, we tend to doubt Jesus. We may not doubt his lordship, but his commitment to give us what we want when we want it is less than firm. The strange thing is that while we doubt Jesus's answers to our questions and prayers, we rarely stop to consider the surety of our own questions and prayers. Perhaps the Jesus we have assumed is not the Jesus who actually is.

If the Jesus who actually exists is different from what we have assumed, our assumptions may need refining. That refining will not come from us because the god of our assumptions lives to serve our desires. Why would we refine our god if we would have to refine our desires? Our desires have become paramount. We have claimed the throne. But the throne is already occupied.

So what does Jesus think of this? What is he doing in this time? We know he is sovereign. We know he is good. We know he is the Creator. He is the King. But what on earth is he doing here? Doesn't he realize how this looks? The Jesus PR and marketing firms must have been getting concerned about their sponsorships.

This is an important statement: Jesus is more after our obedience than our applause. He knows our greatest good is not our comfort but his glory. Jesus gives life and light. We often take this for granted until it is contrasted with darkness and death. Jesus will put our applause, our comfort, and our vision (which are not bad things) on the altar to bring about our worship, his glory, and our joy. He will sacrifice good things for the sake of greater things.

Make no mistake. No matter the situation, Jesus is not idle in working all things for good for those who love him and are called by him. He was not idle in the case of Mary, Martha, and Lazarus. Here we see Jesus also has an accusation, an assumption, and an admission.

Jesus's accusation: *I lost.* This was intentional. Jesus waited. No one made him. Jesus decided when to go despite those who objected. He let Lazarus die. PR is not Jesus's greatest concern. He knows how this looks. He knows the people's thoughts. Jesus says, *I lost to death.*

But we must see Jesus's assumption. *I will not lose.* This is his purpose here. It is revealed in his conversation with Martha. Jesus makes clear, "I am the resurrection and the life. Whoever believes in me, though he die, yet shall he live, and everyone who lives and believes in me shall never die. Do you believe this?"

In other words, Jesus says what they have pronounced as finished is not finished until he says it is finished. And make no mistake. He will say when it is finished.

Jesus is not fazed when the disciples object. He isn't fazed when Martha accuses him. Jesus understands the pressure and the weight, and he is utterly confident because he knows who he is. He knows what he is about to do. God is no stranger to the weight of his own glory. It is his joy in revealing it. He derives gladness from equipping his disciples with it as well.

This raises another intriguing question. If Jesus was so confident and even glad, why did he cry? We have seen Jesus's accusation and assumption. But his admission comes through verse 35, which says, "Jesus wept."

I want to read this as Jesus admitting that maybe he went too far. Maybe he pushed too much on a sore spot in a sore situation. I want him to admit that he can be too big sometimes. I want Jesus to admit that he cries with us, yearns for us, and feels for us. I want Jesus to admit that when I cry, it makes him cry.

Is that his admission here? Yes and no. "When Jesus saw her weeping, and the Jews who had come with her also weeping, he was deeply moved in his spirit and greatly troubled. And he said, 'Where have you laid him?' They said to him, 'Lord, come and see.' Jesus wept" (John 11:33–35).

We might picture different things when we consider the word *wept*. The word used here is not that he metaphorically wept or was simply sad. From John's word choice, he wants us to know literal tears ran down Jesus's face. The Son of God sobbed. Jesus wept.

But why? John tells us it's because when he saw everything going on, he was deeply moved in his spirit and greatly troubled. So what does it mean that he was deeply moved and greatly troubled? Our different English translations will translate these words differently. Your version may have different words for "deeply moved" and "greatly troubled."

The Greek word John uses is *embrimaomai* (em-bri-ma-om-ai), which literally means "sternly warning or scolding." It carries a connotation of anger, outrage, and indignation. The image used is a horse snorting, determined to run and warning all who stand in his way.

In light of this word, it is important to note Jesus is not feeling scolded or warned. Rather Jesus's own spirit is warning and scolding. The question is this: At what is this *embrimaomai* directed? Is it at Martha? Perhaps Mary or the crowd? R. C. Sproul puts his thoughts eloquently as he muses,

> Personally, I think that which caused the anger of the Son of God to boil up and overflow in His spirit was that He was in the presence of the ravaging destruction of the greatest enemy of mankind, death. This was His enemy. This was the foe that, in only a few days, He was going to confront head on in the throes of agony He would experience on the cross, dying to conquer death. Sometimes when I go to the hospital and I see people suffering with cancer, I walk out and say, "I hate cancer!" The affliction is so great and the pain is so enormous. I think this is the kind of visceral reaction Jesus had when He encountered the sorrow that death had provoked. Jesus entered into the affliction of His people so deeply that He was moved within Himself at the travesty of death.[24]

This visceral response reminds me of a scene in C. S. Lewis's classic *The Lion, the Witch, and the Wardrobe,* which is leading up to the culminating event of Aslan laying his life down. After a difficult and decisive conversation between Aslan and the White

Witch in which the great lion agrees to die on behalf of another, Lewis writes,

> At last they heard Aslan's voice, "You can all come back," he said. "I have settled the matter. She has renounced the claim on your brother's blood." The Witch was just turning away with a look of fierce joy on her face when she stopped and said, "But how do I know this promise will be kept?" Aslan ROARED, half rising from his throne; and his great mouth opened wider and wider and the roar grew louder and louder, and the Witch, after staring for a moment with her lips wide apart, picked up her skirts and fairly ran for her life.[25]

At the beginning of this book, we talked about lines of belief. We draw a line and tell Jesus we will go this far, and then he has our trust. But beyond that, we do not believe.

Death had drawn that line. Mary, Martha, and the mourners were all on one side of it. Jesus knew he was about to blow that wide open in a week. As he stared into the wind of his enemy's storm, Jesus grew indignant, filled with a holy rage.

Merrill Tenney states it this way, "Death to Him was not an impassable barrier, but a call to battle."[26]

Jesus's accusation: *I have lost.*

Jesus's assumption: *I will not lose.*

Jesus's admission: *I am in this with you in every way, and I despise death.*

Jesus hates death and everything about it. It is our greatest enemy. In Revelation, we see his final victory over death.

And I heard a loud voice from the throne saying, "Behold, the dwelling place of God is with man. He will dwell with them, and they will be his people, and God himself will be with them as their God. He will wipe away every tear from their eyes, and death shall be no more, neither shall there be mourning, nor crying, nor pain anymore, for the former things have passed away." (Revelation 21:3–4)

I think Jesus is looking at these tears, death, mourning, crying, and pain, and he is thinking, *This is not how it is supposed to be. By my blood I will fix it.* That is where he is headed. On his own accord, he will lose his life. But he is also going to raise it. With it, he will raise you and me. The serpent will bite Jesus's heel (he will lose), but his foot will crush the serpent's head (Genesis 3:15).

He has lost much of the esteem held in the hearts of those who loved him most. He can see it in their eyes. Perhaps he has lost their respect, confidence, sense of security, or trust. Jesus gave death the upper hand. Just as he would on the cross, Jesus is seemingly laying down every temporal opportunity in order to gain an eternal security. Eternal truth trumps momentary perception.

I don't know where you are or what you are facing. It may appear Jesus has lost. But rest in this knowledge: Jesus is still God. He is still able. He will not lose.

As Jesus tells Martha, that is why he came. That is why he is the one who is coming into the world. "I am the resurrection and the life. Whoever believes in me, though he die, yet shall he live, and everyone who lives and believes in me shall never die. Do you believe this?" (John 11:25–26).

Friend, never assume that God is indifferent to suffering. God is not idle when sin is active. It makes him livid. Be careful where you walk. For now we have seen the foreshadowing of Good Friday. Let us now see the foreshadowing of Easter. Let's watch the King in his ultimate victory.

CHAPTER 6

The God Who Raises the Dead

During my freshman year of college, I was in a Christian cover band called The Screaming Bunnies. We would travel around to various youth groups and events and play the popular Christian songs of the day as only we could mess them up.

One of our greatest hits was Chris Rice's, "Cartoon Song". (I know this dates me a bit, but nothing else dated me in college, so it might as well be this.) The song is basically about a variety of cartoon characters and what it would be like if they got saved. The highlight of the verses is when each character sings, "Hallelujah!" in their distinct voice. That was my job. My friend Jeff would sing Chris Rice's part, and I would step to the mic to do the cartoon voices.

There is a long list of characters ranging from Scooby-Doo and Kermit the Frog to Yogi Bear and Fred Flintstone. I did a killer Kermit. However, toward the latter half of the song, Chris Rice sings, "Beavis and that other guy" (because apparently you can't say his real name on Christian radio).

If you are unfamiliar with Beavis and "that other guy," take a second to look them up. They were icons of the MTV generation and were, as my mother put it, "crude and stupid."

After Chris Rice sings, "Beavis and that other guy," there is a pause as the band stops for dramatic effect, waiting for their "Hallelujah." Instead Rice gives a hearty, "Nah!" The band keeps playing, and the youth group kids clap their hands and laugh.

Everyone loved that part, but it always bothered me. Why do we write Beavis and "that other guy" off as beyond saving? I get that we are talking about cartoons. They aren't real. But what does it tell us about our Christian faith that we as a Christian community would cheer, celebrate, clap along with, and affirm this *nah*?

This reveals a subtle undercurrent about how we approach the way God does his work in our world. We love a God who loves what we love. But what if God should stretch across the tracks or into the corners of our personal closets he's not allowed to touch? At that point, could God? Would God? Should God? *Nah—*

We have talked about the God who waits. We have considered the God who gives doubt and the God who loses. In this chapter we are going to consider *the God who raises the dead.* Immediately you see one of these things is not like the others. After all, the God who raises the dead, that's a good thing! We like that. We are on board with that. We believe in that God.

It becomes trickier, however, when we consider not if he is a God who *can* raise the dead but if he is a God who *should.*

We are going to examine the God who raises the dead by looking at John 11:38–44. This is the climactic scene of the passage. When you mention John 11 or talk about the story of Lazarus, this is immediately where your mind goes.

As he describes the scene, Calvin states, "Christ does not come to the tomb as an idle spectator, but like a wrestler preparing for the contest."[27] *Yeah!*

Frederick Bruner describes it this way: "An immovable object meets an irresistible force—Death meets Christ. And Christ conquers."[28] *Yeah!*

Jesus has stacked the deck against himself. The disciples have questioned his timing and place. Mary, Martha, and the mourners have given their accusations, assumptions, and admissions. Finally we come to Jesus standing face-to-face with a closed tomb, surrounded by people who are doubting, questioning, angry, laughing, and embarrassed for Jesus.

We are going to walk through this robust text at a mildly brisk pace, addressing a few side questions along the way. We will press the pause button and give quick answers to quick questions, but I don't want us to get sidetracked. There is a very important point to this entire account. It is something we certainly do not want to miss. The point is the glory of God.

Let's pick up what these verses are telling us and consider how they point us to a big idea. At the end there is a big question for us to face.

"Then Jesus, deeply moved again, came to the tomb. It was a cave, and a stone lay against it" (John 11:38–44). Tombs in that day were either dug out places in rock or caves. Usually there were three places cut into the rock or cave on each side and two in the back. This gave a total of eight spots to lay people to rest. John tells us this tomb was in a cave. Were there other dead people in the cave? We don't know. Regardless, John does tell us there is a large round stone rolled over the entryway.

"Jesus said, 'Take away the stone.' Martha, the sister of the dead man, said to him, 'Lord, by this time there will be an odor, for he has been dead four days'" (John 11:39). There is something interesting here about Martha. Jump back a few verses where the Scripture says,

> Martha said to him, "I know that he will rise again in the resurrection on the last day."
> Jesus said to her, "I am the resurrection and the life. Whoever believes in me, though he die, yet shall he live, and everyone who lives and believes in me shall never die. Do you believe this?"
> She said to him, "Yes, Lord; I believe that you are the Christ, the Son of God, who is coming into the world." (John 11:24–27)

Remember, Martha is the one in our previous chapter who admitted Jesus was still able. He is still the Christ, the Son of God. He is still in control. He still comes through, even though he seemingly didn't come through for her here.

Martha is not questioning whether Jesus *could* raise Lazarus from the dead. Martha is questioning whether he *should*. After all, why in her mind would Jesus want to go in? To see Lazarus one more time? To pay his respects? In her mind she is probably thinking, *Genius, you should have done that four days ago before he died when you could have prevented this whole thing to begin with.*

Martha has an objection. She has legitimate reasons why Jesus should not open the tomb. *It's done. Jesus, you missed the boat.*

It's too messy. This is an embarrassment. Why dig up old scars? Just let it lie, Jesus. There is an odor there.

"Jesus said to her, 'Did I not tell you that if you believed you would see the glory of God?'" (John 11:40). Notice, this sentence is not mentioned previously in our text. So when did Jesus say this to Martha? In verses 25 to 26, he says he is the resurrection and the life, but he is not really talking directly about his glory there. Maybe the messengers in verse 4 brought back the message that this does not lead to death but is for the glory of God so that the Son of God may be glorified through it. That could be what Jesus is referring to.

Perhaps it is simply something they talked about before as a regular topic of conversation. Jesus was likely often telling his followers that by believing in him, they would have life in his name. Having life in Jesus's name is ultimately seeing the glory of God on display here and now in our daily lives. Either way, Jesus makes it clear. This situation is for God's glory. That is the purpose.

"So they took away the stone. And Jesus lifted up his eyes and said, 'Father, I thank you that you have heard me. I knew that you always hear me, but I said this on account of the people standing around, that they may believe that you sent me'" (John 11:41–42). This is not a book about Trinitarian relationship or theology. Neither is this a focus on the prayer life of Jesus. Both are interesting, worthy, and noble pursuits, but for the sake of our conversation, we will not get sidetracked here.

But we do have a few interesting notes concerning Jesus and prayer that we should consider. Listen to what these men have said about what this text tells us about Jesus and prayer. R. H.

Fuller said, "Jesus lives in constant prayer and communication with his Father. When he engages in vocal prayer, he is not entering, as we do, from a state of non-praying into prayer. That is why the prayer is thanksgiving rather than petition."[29] Frederick Bruner said, "Notice, too, that Lazarus, 'who is but meters away in the tomb,' is not even mentioned in Jesus's prayer, as though Jesus does not have to be particularly specific because the Father knows the name and situation."[30] And William Tenney said, "He offered thanks before seeing any results."[31]

Jesus's prayer flows out of a life in constant relationship with God. It is short, simple, and informative for us. Jesus's prayer is one of

- relationship ("Father"),
- thanksgiving ("I thank you that you have heard me"),
- confidence in God ("I knew that you always hear me"),
- mindfulness of others ("I said this on account of the people standing around"), and
- focus on God's glory ("that they may believe that you sent me").

This is not a prescriptive model prayer like the Lord's Prayer is, but it is something to note and take into consideration in order to inform our own prayer lives.

Jesus says the point of this situation is the revealing of the glory of God. In this and every situation pointing to the glory of God, Jesus has an unshaking relationship and confidence in God the Father in order to accomplish the overarching goal of his glory.

God's glory does not lose. Jesus's prayer reflects that truth.

"When he had said these things, he cried out with a loud voice, 'Lazarus, come out.' The man who had died came out" (John 11:43). Notice the complete lack of showmanship on the part of Jesus. This is not a wordy or showy miracle. This should lead us to conclude that the point of the miracle is not the miracle. Rather the point is the glory of God. That is Jesus's aim. It is a very focused aim. Jesus is so intent and moved in his spirit that he is short in his command. "Lazarus! Come out!" This is not an invitation. This is an order from the master of life and death.

John gives us something else interesting here. Who does he say came out of the tomb? We know it is Lazarus, but John doesn't say, "Lazarus." John instead calls him, "The man who had died."

There is a new identity to this man. He is no longer just Lazarus. From this point on, no one will separate Lazarus from his miraculous conversion from death to life. No longer would he be who he was. He is now the man who died, the man who was raised to life by the glory of God. That is what our God does. He changes identity.

"The man who had died came out, his hands and feet bound with linen strips, and his face wrapped with a cloth. Jesus said to them, 'Unbind him, and let him go'" (John 11:44). So how did Lazarus get out of the cave if he was bound? This is a question a lot of people like to wrestle with concerning this passage. The answer? We don't know. Some say the Jews did not wrap tightly like the Egyptians did. Rather, not fearing mummies, they wrapped more loosely. Some say the body was wrapped, but the arms of the deceased were still free. Some speculate that Jesus miraculously brought him to the door.

Again we don't know. It is important to remember we are talking about Jesus having raised a man from the dead. Let's not get too caught up on how he got to the door. That is not important here.

What is important is Jesus's command, "Unbind him. Let him go!" We need to note Jesus does not only have one command in this passage. He has two. Both commands are gloriously weighty calls. The first is directed to Lazarus. "Come out!" But the job is not done there. Jesus calls to the people, "Unbind him. Let him go!"

Why did Jesus need to tell them to unbind him? Or to ask it another way, why is Lazarus staying bound? There is probably one of two answers. Either everyone rushed to see the spectacle, so overwhelmed with the mummy Lazarus that they forgot about the person inside, or nobody rushed to him because of fear. They wanted to see it; they just didn't want to touch it.

Imagine yourself among that crowd. There he stands. The man who was dead is now alive. The wrappings rise and fall as his very lungs take in and breath out the odor-filled air of which Martha had cautioned Jesus. What would you have done? Would you have ran up to get a closer look? Would you have poked his arms or his face to see if what you were seeing was actually real? Perhaps you would stay back, knowing this had just gotten all too real and you were not touching that with a ten-foot pole.

I think I would go ... after you and a few people went first.

Either way, they are all looking at him astounded. They have witnessed the miracle of life. But there is still more to do. God's glory didn't simply come and go when Lazarus was raised. There was still work for people to participate in.

Jesus calls the crowd to see Lazarus, to touch him and move forward with him. *Unbind him and let him go!*

This is an amazing story. If anything is miraculous, this story is. But I've seen a dead person raised. I have. I have been in this situation as an observer. I can relate.

Her name was Sarah. We were in the same class in high school. That being said, we were in very different classes in high school. She was a cheerleader. She was popular, attractive, everything the stereotypical *it* girl was.

I was president of the debate team. A youth group kid.

While we both attended the same church, we went to very different churches. Hers was one where you went on Sundays, but it was more of a social outing. Her parents were wonderful, caring Christians. Sarah wanted to stay in the good graces of the parents so she would get dressed up for a few hours and paint on that religious smile.

She also went to our church's youth camps. Along with her, she would bring her cheerleader friends. This obviously resulted in a herd of nominal, testosterone-filled, popular, good-looking, football-playing guys tagging along as well. This made it really awkward for me and the few other guys who were active at the church but were not part of that group.

All of a sudden, we as a same-grade class had to sit together. We had to share with one another. We had to share bathrooms with one another. We hid under our sleeping bags as they slapped each other with towels. We had to pretend we liked one another, even though we all knew that come August, when the school bell rang, they were on one side of the hall and we were on the other.

They might even stick around church for a few weeks, depending on how much they had cried at camp. But after a short while, things would settle back down to normal. They had their Friday and Saturday nights back. We had our Wednesday nights and Sunday mornings back.

This unspoken agreement worked until one year when Sarah kept coming long after the others had dropped off. Not only that, but she was cutting ties with some of her old habits and circles of influence tied to those habits.

In the youth group, we were glad about this for a while. The youth group girls would talk with her and sit with her. After a while she was coming by herself. She talked as though she had been actually reading, wrestling with, and applying the principles of the Bible to her life. She was being questioned and interacting less at school with her group, but she was still held at arm's length by our youth group. We had seen this story before. We were skeptical.

Then something else happened—lunch. We all remember the political zoo-like atmosphere of high school lunch. *You have this booth. We have this table. You have that corner, etc.*

One day Sarah quit sitting at the popular table. Sarah didn't even move to the Christian kid table. Sarah started sitting at the leftover table. The leftovers were those who didn't sit with anybody and by default sat with one another, yet they didn't talk to one another either because that would be classified as socialization. They were a different group, the group of loners.

Sarah sat there, but not out of necessity. She started sitting there and befriending people. Over time she was gradually more and more accepted in our Christian group at church, but then she crossed a line. She started bringing these loners. She was buying them Bibles and giving them rides, and it almost looked ... intentional.

Honestly this made us uncomfortable. *They are from the other side of the tracks. They are the spoiled kids. They are the outcasts. They are the drunks. They just don't fit here. They are the dead ones. We are the living ones, and we kind of like it that way. Sarah, you keep pushing the door back on that tomb, and it's just going to get smellier and smellier in here.*

We knew Sarah was a dead person. She had it all, so we tried to give her none of what we had. She was wrapped up in the course of this world. We had found the narrow path. She was living it up now. We had eyes focused on eternity.

When she and her cute, popular cheerleader friends would come into contact with us as the church, we were cautious. *I know you can, God, but I doubt you will. I know how this story goes.*

When she kept coming, we grew uncomfortable. *God, what are you doing? We're glad she's here. She's popular! This kind of makes us look good. But this is upsetting the balance. God, you don't really save people like Sarah. They've already got it all.*

When she kept bringing new people, we reached a new level. *The last thing we need is more of these people. This is a church!*

I don't know exactly how it happened—her coming to life. All I know is Jesus saved her. She and I had many conversations about God, Christ, salvation, and various other topics for many years. We became good friends.

Here is how I would explain Sarah's testimony to you as an observer—as I saw it with my own eyes. Sarah was dead. God spoke life into her and saved her. He brought her forward and said to us, "Unbind her. Let her go," and we were hesitant. We had doubt. We were uncomfortable with the proceedings.

God used Sarah to reveal a startling truth. In this case, Sarah was the one seeing the glory of God, and we were the ones who were dead. We knew God could raise Sarah from the dead, but we didn't think he would. We weren't even sure if he really should.

What do you believe God could raise but shouldn't?

How is your marriage? *It's going great. You know I'd love to be that Ephesians 5 husband, but my wife is no Proverbs 31 woman, if you know what I mean. Besides, do you know how that conversation would go? How long it would take? Do you know how deep we would have to dig, how it might smell, how it might look? It would be embarrassing. Jesus, you can, but you probably shouldn't.*

How are your friends? *Good, doing good. I'm still praying for them. I know God can do it! But by all means, I can't step in. We have a good working relationship. Things are civil. There must be another way. They would make people nervous. God, save them. You can, but if you do, let me know when it's done.*

How is your relationship with God? *Great (#blessed)! Just staying positive. You know, love, love, love. But I don't want to really follow Christ. I will give him my heart but not my obedience. I struggle just to actually read the Bible, much less apply and wrestle with it. God, just raise me on that day! I have my card punched. I walked an aisle. I said a prayer. I don't want to go to hell. I just want to live like it until I get to heaven. God, just raise me on the last day. But God, if I let you go there now, it's going to stink. It's too far gone. It is dead. I prefer it dead.*

God, don't challenge me. Just comfort me. Don't yell at me to come alive. Just hold me in my death. I would rather stay dead than put in the effort it takes to be alive.

We could go on and on, but you know what I'm talking about. It is different for each of us, but at its core it is the same. We assume we are alive apart from the Holy Spirit's work of pushing us toward being Christlike. Trading current life for a different life plus religiosity just doesn't sound appealing. But that is not what the Holy Spirit does. God calls us not to religious adaptation but to complete gospel transformation.

I believe it was Woody Allen who once said, "I'm not afraid to die. I just don't want to be there when it happens." This is how many of us feel about the process of sanctification. We are on board with being Christlike as an idea but uncomfortable with it as a pursuit. We think hating hell and other people's sin is enough. We don't really want to have to love and wrestle with an intrusive Holy Spirit.

Lying in green pastures beside still waters with a restored soul—that's the path we believe in. That is the goal. But when that path starts into the valley of the shadow, we grow concerned with where it could be headed.

I have actually heard someone say, "Well, Jesus loves me, and if he loves me, he wouldn't want me to die." This was in a conversation about missions. I assume this person must also believe the beloved apostles are still living in a condo in south Florida.

I am not telling you to adopt a death wish. I am telling you that you will need to die to become like Christ. You will need to die to your purposes, kingdom, pride, and sense of self-exaltation. You will need to take up your cross and follow Jesus to where death happens. If not, life will not happen. If you are never marked as "the man who had died," then you can never be the person who has been raised by Christ.

Sin is not meant to be hidden but violently murdered. It is to be whipped, mocked, stripped, exposed, nailed to wood, and have a spear stuck in its side until it is unequivocally dead. This is a very different idea than sanctification as represented in the majority of our Christian culture.

Many of our songs, books, and really lame T-shirts convey the idea that gospel transformation is more a shift in mood, demeanor, or outlook. We talk about being positive, encouraging, peaceful, and many other fine adjectives, but these can be accomplished apart from the cross of Christ. There are many sunshiny, positive, affirming atheists. None of them are saved. Salvation requires death—Jesus's death and your death.

But as Jesus said, the endgame is not death but the glory of God.

> Do you not know that the unrighteous will not inherit the kingdom of God? Do not be deceived: neither the sexually immoral, nor idolaters, nor adulterers, nor men who practice homosexuality, nor thieves, nor the greedy, nor drunkards, nor revilers, nor swindlers will inherit the kingdom of God. And such were some of you. But you were washed, you were sanctified, you were justified in the name of the Lord Jesus Christ and by the Spirit of our God. (1 Corinthians 6:9–11)

And you were dead in the trespasses and sins in which you once walked, following the course of this world, following the prince of the power of the air, the spirit that is now at work in the sons of disobedience—among whom we all once lived in the passions of our flesh, carrying out the desires of the body and the mind, and were by nature children of wrath, like the rest of mankind.

But God, being rich in mercy, because of the great love with which he loved us, even when we were dead in our trespasses, made us alive together with Christ—by grace you have been saved—and raised us up with him and seated us with him in the heavenly places in Christ Jesus, so that in the coming ages he might show the immeasurable riches of his grace in kindness toward us in Christ Jesus.

For by grace you have been saved through faith. And this is not your own doing; it is the gift of God, not a result of works, so that no one may boast. For we are his workmanship, created in Christ Jesus for good works, which God prepared beforehand, that we should walk in them. (Ephesians 2:1–9)

This is the glory of God. This is the gospel. God is a God who will raise the dead, is raising the dead, and has raised the dead in Christ. We are all dead apart from Christ. We are just dead in different ways. But in his grace God has saved, is saving, and will save some of us.

"Did I not tell you that if you believed, you would see the glory of God?" (John 11:40). This is the big question—the apex where all of this is pointing. Do you want to see the glory of God? Yes or no?

Friend, you have to make a decision. If you don't, you have already made the decision. The glory of God is messy, and the longer something is dead, the messier it is going to be in bringing it to life. Jesus said, "I am the resurrection and the life. Whoever believes in me, though he die, yet shall he live, and everyone who lives and believes in me shall never die. Do you believe this?" John Macarthur states,

> The Lord promised [Martha] that if she would believe she would see the glory of God revealed. That did not, of course, make the miracle dependent on her faith. It was a sovereign act of Christ, designed to glorify Himself and the Father by putting His resurrection power on display. Consequently it would have happened no matter how Martha had responded. But though all present would see the miracle, only those who had faith in Christ would see the fullness of God's glory reflected in it.[32]

If you want to see the glory of God, you don't need another miracle. You don't need another big event. Quit waiting for another program. You want to see the glory of God? Believe Jesus is the Christ, the Son of God, and by believing, you can have life in his name. Walk in obedience in every area of your resurrected life. Have a God-filled, glory-filled Tuesday. Stick close to Jesus, because he is the life and only he can resurrect. His life through his resurrection is his glory for us in Christ Jesus.

Here's the take-home question: Where is God shouting for life in you? In your family? At your job? In your church?

Instead of telling God why he shouldn't, what if we said this: *God, whatever you do, I will unbind and let go. You do the saving. You do the raising. And I'll do whatever you call me to do. It may be messy, long, or embarrassing. It may break the veneer I've worked so hard to keep polished. But I trust that if it happens, I will see the glory of God. I want to see the glory of God.*

Until you get to that place, you will not see the glory of God. God is a God who receives glory by raising the dead. It is the story of the gospel. It is my story. In some areas I am still unbinding and letting go. In some areas, if I'm being honest, I'm still persuading Jesus why he shouldn't get involved.

Believers are ones who roll away stones continually. Lost people are ones who won't. It is that simple.

This is a difficult truth. This truth created a tension that got Jesus killed.

CHAPTER 7

The God Who Creates Tension

When I was in fifth grade at Woodlands Elementary School in Ponca City, Oklahoma, there was a game of thrones. It was a battle of empires between the fifth-grade boys and the sixth-grade boys. It all started when a girl named Jill, a sixth-grader loved and adored by the sixth-grade boys, began to fancy my friend Aaron, a fifth-grade boy. They had been passing notes and talking at recess, and there had even been rumors of a confirmed handholding. This made the sixth-grade boys incredibly upset.

The sixth-grade boys were soccer kids. Behind our school, we had a basketball court. On the other side of the court, there was some playground equipment. Just behind the playground, there was a hill that sloped down to an open field with a backstop. At each recess the sixth-grade boys went down and played soccer in that field.

The fifth-grade boys were basketball kids. Our domain was the blacktop. They had their soccer field, and we had our basketball court. It worked.

It just so happened that shortly after the trysts began to escalate between Jill and Aaron, the sixth-grade boys made a startling move.

One particular Monday, they ran out early and got to the basketball court before us. This was our turf. We let them know in no uncertain terms that we did not appreciate this infringement and that if they continued, there would be consequences. They let us know in no uncertain terms that they did not appreciate our infringement on their sixth-grade girls and that if we continued, there would be consequences. Words came to shoves. Shoves came to fisticuffs. Fisticuffs escalated to a boisterous scuffle that was quickly broken up by the monitoring teachers.

Over the course of the next several days, we fifth-grade boys became master military strategists. Only one grade could rule this school, and it would not be those Umbro-wearing, Adidas-cleated little punks.

That Friday, we set our plan in place. We scarfed down our lunch and all met at the back wall of the school overlooking the basketball court. Both groups had been banned from the basketball court, so it stood as a vacant lot where tumbleweeds rolled swiftly by as if they were seeking to escape the ensuing tumult.

The sixth grade boys went down to their soccer field as usual, unaware. At the stroke of 12:15, a cry went up—a high-pitched prepubescent cry. Like William Wallace's Scots raging down upon the English militants of King Edward I, we attacked with raging, violent, tiny fists.

What we had was a tension between two perceived kingdoms. It was a battle over power, dominance, and the one throne. This metaphor applies as we turn to our final chapter. Throughout the next few pages, we are going to look at a power struggle that creates tension in each of us. It is a tension that grew continually as Jesus displayed his power and claim as the Christ, the Son of God.

The last God we don't believe in is *the God who creates tension.* Hopefully we have felt tension in our beliefs and assumptions over the course of our time together, leading up to the raising of Lazarus. However, here we see that event is merely a catalyst, a breaking point. It is merely the beginning of a great fallout John exposes in chapters 11 through 19 of his book, ultimately culminating in Jesus's resurrection in chapters 20 and 21.

This result should be surprising to us. After Lazarus was raised and Jesus gives his echoing command, "Unbind him and let him go," we expect the words, "And they all lived happily ever after." The end.

The fact that there is more of a fallout should be shocking to us. I didn't know there were options as to how to regard a man who just raised someone from the dead. If I see you raise a dead person, I give up. You win. Whatever you want, it's yours. This seems like a pretty cut and dried scenario to me.

But hopefully you have begun to see as we have walked through John 11, this is not a story about Jesus raising a dead man. This is an account *in which* Jesus raises a dead man but is about so much more. After all, it wasn't what Jesus did that created the tension. It was what he claimed his actions meant. He said they showed he was God.

In the last leg of our journey, we are going to look at what John tells us in John 11:45–12:11. It begins with a very important word—*therefore.* This *therefore* is going to send us on a journey through the text. As we walk through the text, we will look at some commentary, seeking to set ourselves in the context and be immersed in the story.

It is important for us to understand the different lenses through which Jesus raising Lazarus from the dead is seen.

God's glory always creates a light. In order to get a broad spectrum of this light, we will look through the lenses of three key people, specifically Caiaphas, Judas, and Mary. In light of Jesus revealing God's glory, we will see their risk, reason, and result. I pray for open eyes and hearts as we are faced with the very real, very uncomfortable reality of a God who creates tension.

"Many of the Jews therefore, who had come with Mary and had seen what he did, believed in him, but some of them went to the Pharisees and told them what Jesus had done" (John 11:45–46). Before we consider our three figures, we need to set some context. Let's rewind and recall what is on the other side of this *therefore* in verse 45. After he was almost killed and arrested for blasphemy in Jerusalem, Jesus goes across the Jordan River. While he is there, he is told that his friend Lazarus is ill. Jesus waits until Lazarus is dead. He lets him die. Then despite the stern warning and caution of his disciples, he goes back to the area where he was almost killed. He shows up four days too late. Amidst a cloud of controversy, Jesus is accused by his closest friends. Not only that, but this is all done in front of many of the same people who saw him almost killed for blasphemy when he claimed to be God.

Jesus raises Lazarus from the dead and says the whole event has been done to display the glory of God.

> So the chief priests and the Pharisees gathered the council and said, "What are we to do? For this man performs many signs. If we let him go on like this, everyone will believe in him, and the Romans will come and take away both our place and our nation." But one of them, Caiaphas, who was high priest that year, said to them, "You know nothing at all. Nor do you understand that it is better for you that one man should die for the people, not that the whole nation should perish." (John 11:47–50)

Remember earlier when I said those of you who prefer books over movies would be frustrated by this text because John is giving the action without the behind-the-scenes thought, emotion, and purpose? Here's the good news: John begins to do that here. He starts peeling back the curtain to unveil the realities behind every thought and action. "He did not say this of his own accord, but being high priest that year he prophesied that Jesus would die for the nation, and not for the nation only, but also to gather into one the children of God who are scattered abroad" (John 11:51–52).

In order to clarify, John tells us Caiaphas said this prophecy unknowingly or "not of his own accord." Note the sovereignty of God displayed here even in the murderous words of evil men. "So from that day on they made plans to put him to death. Jesus therefore no longer walked openly among the Jews, but went from there to the region near the wilderness, to a town called Ephraim [just a few miles north of Jerusalem], and there he stayed with the disciples" (John 11:53–57).

Jesus in essence has become an outlaw at this point.

> Now the Passover of the Jews was at hand, and many went up from the country to Jerusalem before the Passover to purify themselves. They were looking for Jesus and saying to one another as they stood in the temple, "What do you think? That he will not come to the feast at all?" Now the chief priests and the Pharisees had given orders that if anyone knew where he was, he should let them know, so that they might arrest him. (John 11:55–57)

It is estimated that more than a million people converged on Jerusalem during the Passover. During this electric time, listen to the major topic of conversation: *Did you hear Jesus raised a guy from the dead? I know! I heard he almost got killed a few weeks ago. Do you think he'll come back?*

Indeed, it was likely Jesus would come back. After all, he was a Jew, and this was the Passover. The Passover was a marvelous celebration. It included a tremendous feast to remember the Jewish captivity in Egypt and God's miraculous deliverance. They know Jesus will show ... unless he is scared, unless he has decided this whole "Hey, I'm God!" thing is a complete charade not worth the cost.

There is a thickness in the air with rumors, predictions, assumptions, and speculations all surrounding the next move of Jesus, the supposed Messiah.

Despite what the Jewish people think Jesus will do, we do know the chief priests and the Pharisees believe he will come.

They have all eyes out. They've recruited spies and bounty hunters to set a trap for Jesus.

> Six days before the Passover, Jesus therefore came to Bethany, where Lazarus was, whom Jesus had raised from the dead.
>
> So they gave a dinner for him there. Martha served, and Lazarus was one of those reclining with him at table.
>
> Mary therefore took a pound of expensive ointment made from pure nard, and anointed the feet of Jesus and wiped his feet with her hair. The house was filled with the fragrance of the perfume.
>
> But Judas Iscariot, one of his disciples (he who was about to betray him), said, "Why was this ointment not sold for three hundred denarii and given to the poor?"
>
> He said this, not because he cared about the poor, but because he was a thief, and having charge of the moneybag he used to help himself to what was put into it.
>
> Jesus said, "Leave her alone, so that she may keep it [or she has kept it] for the day of my burial. For the poor you always have with you, but you do not always have me." (John 12:1–8)

Before we go much further, let's set the picture. This dinner was no small event. In fact, Matthew and Mark also include this account in their gospel letters (Matthew 26:2; Mark 14:3). Specifically they say the dinner took place at the house of Simon the Leper. Who was Simon the Leper? Well, his name was Simon, and he was a leper. The key word here is *was*. This is like calling Lazarus "the man who *was* dead."

Simon is someone who has also been given a new identity in Christ. He was no longer a leper. He had been healed at some point. We know this because people would never have gathered in the home of someone with an active disease like leprosy. Not only would they have feared getting the disease, but merely being around him would have made them ceremonially unclean just before the Passover.

At Simon the Leper's house, we have a unique dinner scene. The dinner guests are likely sitting at a U-shaped table. There are at least seventeen people (Jesus, his twelve disciples, Mary, Martha, Lazarus, and Simon) all reclining around a table that is low to the floor. People lay down near the table, their feet facing out and their heads pointed toward the table itself. They would have been propped up on one elbow, eating with the other hand.

Picture it—Jesus, a guy who was dead, a former leper, a clan of nervous disciples, and two joy-filled sisters all leaning near one another, splitting some wine, bitter herbs, and flat bread.

> When the large crowd of the Jews learned that Jesus was there, they came, not only on account of him but also to see Lazarus, whom he had raised from the dead. So the chief priests made plans to put Lazarus to death as well, because on account of him many of the Jews were going away and believing in Jesus. (John 12:9–11)

At last we have arrived at the God who creates tension. Tension is defined as anxious feelings, a sense of conflict, a pulling force, strain, pressure, or tightness. If you put tension on something, one of two things is going to eventually happen. Either it will snap and break under the tension, or it will give in and conform to a state of non-tension. Tension exists because of counter wills exerting force on an object until one of them wins.

There really is no third option, especially when it comes to Jesus. Jesus makes this clear as he says in John 3:36, "Whoever believes in the Son has eternal life; whoever does not obey the Son shall not see life, but the wrath of God remains on him." In Luke 11:23, he also says, "Whoever is not with me is against me, and whoever does not gather with me scatters."

Macarthur explains, "Like no one else, Jesus Christ evokes the antithetical extremes of love and hate, devotion and rejection, worship and blasphemy, and faith and unbelief. How people respond to him divides the sheep from the goats; the wheat from the tares; believers from unbelievers; the saved from the lost."[33]

This is why we don't believe in a God who creates tension. Mainly we don't like tension. We think God likes us and wants us to be happy. Therefore, he won't give us tension, because tension makes us unhappy.

We are masters of escaping conflict. While I was working on this chapter, I went to the Amazon.com book category and typed in "conflict avoidance." More than 6,500 unique titles were listed. Out of curiosity I typed in "conflict resolution." More than sixty thousand titles were presented. If conflict cannot be avoided, we believe it must be stamped out like a smoldering fire. We do not like tension because tension takes work. Even if we are willing to do the work, it is often the quickest resolution or path of least resistance we are likely to take.

Not only do we avoid conflict, but we have issues of control as well. We like to think we have options. We are the initiators and deciders. We sit on the throne and dictate. We will not be dictated to. After all, we believe God's job is to get us out of tension and to make us feel better. Wasn't that the point of the cross? So we can do whatever we want and Jesus has to pay for it? Why put the pressure on us (sarcasm)?

This is how we know God is a God who creates tension—the Bible. This is the story repeated and repeated throughout Scripture. Out of the overflow of his love, God gives us tension to remind us we are not God. In our sin we want to go one way, and in his grace and by his Spirit, God aligns us in another.

We believe God exists to serve us. God knows we exist to serve him. The gospel creates tension. R. C. Sproul observes,

> Every time the gospel has been proclaimed boldly and accurately in church history, there has been persecution. Every time the church speaks out to confront ungodliness in the culture, there is a backlash. I have no desire to go looking for persecution and conflict, but the fact that I live so free of persecution makes me question my commitment to the things of God. I don't like conflict, but I hate to stand among people like Caiaphas.[34]

That is why Jesus causes tension in this passage. Verse 48 is our dead giveaway. The religious leaders want a place. They want a nation. They want a God. Just not that place, not that nation, not that God.

What is the result of this tension? We can summarize the tension response by looking at three people under this tension and how they respond. Let's begin with Caiaphas as a representative of the chief priests and religious leaders.

> So the chief priests and the Pharisees gathered the council and said, "What are we to do? For this man performs many signs. If we let him go on like this, everyone will believe in him, and the Romans will come and take away both our place and our nation." But one of them, Caiaphas, who was high priest that year, said to them, "You know nothing at all. Nor do you understand that it is better for you that one man should die for the people, not that the whole nation should perish." (John 11:47–50)

John 11:57 then says, "Now the chief priests and the Pharisees had given orders that if anyone knew where he was, he should let them know, so that they might arrest him." John 12:10–11 states, "So the chief priests made plans to put Lazarus to death as well, because on account of him many of the Jews were going away and believing in Jesus."

What a fun bunch! Caiaphas and the chief priests are the very definition of the word *antagonists*. They are set against Jesus to the full extent of their power and reach. They want him dead.

Why? They believe in God and the Messiah. Why not at least investigate? Why not ask themselves the question, "Could this be the Christ, the Son of God?" The response of these men reminds us of Jesus's words in Luke 16:31, which says, "If they do not hear Moses and the Prophets, neither will they be convinced if someone should rise from the dead."

Caiaphas and the chief priests point us to an important truth. The cause of unbelief is not inadequate information. It's a heart in rebellion against God, a heart set against his authority and his glory. This is the source of the tension.

Tension arises from a sense of danger, a feeling something is at risk. To grasp Caiaphas's mind-set, we must consider what is at risk for him. If he feels a threat from Jesus, what exactly is being threatened that is worth defending to the point of murder?

John tells us, "Caiaphas was high priest that year." This is true. Actually Caiaphas was high priest for eighteen years. Priests were supposed to serve in their position for life according to the Old Testament law. However, under Roman rule, priests were merely figureheads of power. Rome could replace them and often did so if anything was perceived to be askew. Religiously Caiaphas had his office. Politically it was up for debate. You don't stay in politics for eighteen years unless you are a good politician. The office of high priest had become a very political position.

Jesus is a threat to Caiaphas's sense of security. That is what is at risk. The priests betray themselves. "If we let him go on like this, everyone will believe in him." Why would that be so bad? Is it that he obviously is not God? Is he leading the people of God astray? Have they found some fault with him they must expose? No, their reasoning is not rooted in any of these justifications. Rather it is rooted in the fear that Rome would sense unrest and come take away both their place, the symbol of their authority and privilege, their nation, their designation, their reputation, and their recognition as God's leaders.

God's glory in Christ was a threat to their security. It stood in the way of their ultimate goal—power. What is the reason or the excuse they hide behind? *It's for the good of the people. You don't want the nation to perish, do you? You don't hate the nation or the temple, do you? Do you want to be the cause of this mess? Do you want the spears of Rome pointed at your head? No, it is best for the sake of the people that we stay in control. For us to stay in control, this man has to die.*

Sin is a cancerous sickness. Not only does Caiaphas intend to murder Jesus since in his mind it is "better that one man die for the sake of the people," but by the end of verse 10, he has two people lined up to die. This is what sin does. It protects the empire of the self at all costs. It multiplies itself. Sin publicly stands against the glory of God under the pretense of providing good for the self or others.

What is at risk for Caiaphas? His security. What is his reason? The nation. What is Caiaphas's result under tension? He snaps under the weight and pull of his own glory.

While Caiaphas was a major player in the plot to capture and murder Jesus, Judas is perhaps best known as his betrayer.

> But Judas Iscariot, one of his disciples (he who was about to betray him), said, "Why was this ointment not sold for three hundred denarii and given to the poor?" He said this, not because he cared about the poor, but because he was a thief, and having charge of the moneybag he used to help himself to what was put into it. (John 12:4–6)

Of all the people in this account, Judas has the easiest road. Some people are getting curveballs, some fastballs, but Judas is playing T-ball. The man is one of Jesus's handpicked twelve disciples. He is with Jesus every day. He has seen every miracle and heard every sermon. He has had every opportunity to ask every question.

If anyone with a heart of rebellion would relent to Jesus and his glory, it should be Judas. Yet here he sees a surpassingly beautiful, sacrificial act of worship, and he calls it an extravagant waste.

What is at risk for Judas? His secret sin. Judas's secret was that he was a thief. John tells us in verse 6 that he used to take for himself out of the money bag meant for ministry. But beneath this secret was the secret sin of selfishness.

Here Jesus puts so much tension on Judas's secret sin it causes him to boil. *Why not take this and put it in the money bag? Why waste this on Jesus? This is not going to benefit me. Why should Jesus get the public glory when I can receive the secret wealth? Why praise in this way at this time? It's too much. It's outward. It's showy, and it's too much for this man. Not only will I not participate, but I will also condemn those who do.*

What is Judas's justification or his reason? Just like Caiaphas, Judas doesn't out and out say it. Rather he conceals his selfish indignation under the disguise of the poor. "The poor need this," Judas says. Judas is lying, and he knows it. He doesn't care about the poor. He cares about his own wealth and his own empire.

Matthew Henry rightly assesses, "Notice the enemies of Christ and his gospel have often colored their enmity with a smug care for the public good and the common safety, and, in order to do this, have branded his prophets and ministers as troublers."[35]

What is at risk for Judas? His secret sin. What is his reasoning? The poor. What is Judas's result under tension? He snaps under the weight and pull of his own glory.

Contrasted with Caiaphas and Judas, we again return to Mary. Remember where we left Mary in verse 32? She was at Jesus's feet, thrown down in confusion, anger, and fear. Where do we first meet Mary in Luke 10:39? She was at Jesus's feet, learning and asking questions. Now we see her at his feet worshipping. "Mary therefore took a pound of expensive ointment made from pure nard, and anointed the feet of Jesus and wiped his feet with her hair. The house was filled with the fragrance of the perfume" (John 12:3).

To the Jews, washing the feet of another person was for menial slaves. It was a degrading, disgusting job. Not only is Mary doing that here for Jesus, but she also lets down her hair to wash his feet. No respectable Jewish woman would have let down her hair in public. It was considered indecent, immodest, and immoral. No woman with any degree of pride or self-respect would do what Mary is doing here.

To further her sacrificial act of worship, she uses pure nard. What she washes his feet with is extravagant. Nard was a fragrant oil extracted from a plant found in the mountains of northern India. It was very expensive. John notes it cost about a year's wages or three hundred denarii. For comparison today, even at a minimum-wage position, this is equivalent to around fifteen thousand dollars' worth of ointment she is pouring on the feet of Jesus.

William Barclay observes, "Mary took the most precious thing she possessed and spent it all on Jesus. Love is not love if it nicely calculates the cost. It gives its all and its only regret is that it has not still more to give."[36] Mary refused to give Jesus something that cost her nothing. In fact, it may have cost her everything. If not materially everything, certainly it cost her socially.

For the disciples this act is recalling another event that happened previously in Galilee at a Pharisee's house. The account is recorded in Luke 7:36–39. Jesus and the disciples are reclining at table. An adulterous woman, a prostitute, discovers he is there. She goes in with a jar of alabaster and begins weeping, soaking Jesus's feet with her tears. She wipes his feet with her hair (which is presumably already down) and begins anointing him with the ointment.

Here we have sweet Mary making herself like this prostitute. The disciples would have known what she was doing. They would have remembered the event vividly.

Mary displays openly before Jesus the fact that she knows she is no better than a prostitute. She comes to him with nothing but her all—her dignity, her modesty, decency, worship, money, possessions, pride, all of it at the feet of Jesus.

Have you ever done anything like that for Jesus? Not only sat at his feet or thrown yourself down at his feet but laid down your dignity, decency, worship, resources, possessions, everything you have and are at his feet, coming to Jesus like a repentant prostitute?

For Mary, what is at risk is her pride. Her reason is simple repentance. *You are God. I am not. Your glory, not mine. Your kingdom come, your will be done. I abandon me and my empire, and I cling to yours. You are the Christ, the Son of God, and I come seeking life in your name.*

The result for Mary under the pressure of the gospel is that she relents. She succumbs to the glory of God, and it is beautiful.

What a difference between these responses. It is the same tension for all three of them. They are all responding to the glory of God displayed in the same ways, but they are building different mutually exclusive empires.

Concerning those who snap under the relentless tension of the gospel, John Calvin notes, "This is how confident wicked people are. They claim everything for themselves, as if it were in their power to do what they like, and as if even the result of the work depended on their will. They are putting their own energy against God's power, as if by persevering they could be stronger than God in the end."[37]

Do we feel the tension Jesus presents? We should. I pray we do. By God's grace, while we are all dead in our sins, we should hope and pray that we continually feel a drawing, a pull, a tension between our hearts steeped in rebellion and the call toward being Christlike, being transformed by the Spirit. We are strangers, foreigners in a home stained by sin in a way it should not be. It is a way that brought Jesus to such indignant anger and so deeply troubled his spirit that he wept.

Do we weep?

Do we weep over our families, our marriages, our need for power, our secret sin, our love of money, and our discontentment in God's provision? Why, or why not?

Let us conclude our time together with a few questions of self-evaluation. The text we have read raises many questions. It did so for the people in the narrative, and it should for us as well.

Do you consider God's glory a threat?

What is at risk for you? Is it power, secret sin, or pride?

For God's glory to win, to be seen as paramount in your life or circumstance, what has to happen? Are you willing to lay that down?

Some may be wrestling with a simple yet weighty question. Whatever I must lay down, if I lose it, what will I get?

Jesus tells us as he told Martha. *Did I not tell you that if you believe, you will see the glory of God? For whoever would save his life will lose it, but whoever loses his life for my sake, and the gospel's will save it. For what does it profit a man to gain the whole world and forfeit his soul?*

Friend, what you get is Jesus. He is all, and he is enough.

Conclusion

For people who may not like confrontation, we have been confronted with a lot about Jesus over the course of this book. I don't know your reaction to this. As I've heard it said, Jesus came to comfort the afflicted and afflict the comfortable. Right now you are likely finding yourself in one of those two camps.

Regardless of how we feel about the God of the Bible in John 11–12, my prayer is that we will at least seek to understand him as he is—as Jesus Christ, the Son of God, who is displayed openly in Scripture. He is good. He is right. He can be trusted.

If this is a struggle for you, that is okay. I admit that I struggle with God in light of the topics covered in this book as well. It is not a struggle with the sovereignty or goodness of God. My greatest struggle in prayer is rooted in a deep corner of my heart I often don't want to acknowledge exists. Let me be clear. I believe God is good. I believe whatever happens, he can and will use it for his glory and the good of those who are called according to his purposes (Romans 8:28; Genesis 50:20). But still, if I am completely honest, I'm afraid God will hurt me or someone I love.

I know this seems strange. Why would a good God, one identified inseparably with love, want to hurt me or someone I love?

In that deep corner of my heart, there is a fear associated with my faith. While I believe God is good and loving, I know sometimes the most refining element is fire. The strongest way to shape something is to strike it. The loudest voice comes through the most violent megaphone.

C. S. Lewis wrote, "God whispers to us in our pleasures, speaks in our conscience, but shouts in our pains; it is His megaphone to rouse a deaf world."[38] If I stepped back and examined my prayer life, honestly I would find that most of my prayers are pointed toward the avoidance of pain, the comfort of pleasures, and the soundness of a conscience of moral peace. However, according to Lewis, this leaves me only content to hear whispers and the even-keeled voice of a very thunderous Creator God.

This leads me to my point. I believe God is good. I have grown most spiritually in the dry times, the excruciating circumstances, and the painful moments of a broken world colliding with a sinful heart. Pain has been a means of growth by God's grace.

Still, when I find myself praying for spiritual growth, for God to save my son, for my wife and I to radiantly display the gospel in our marriage, for gospel growth in our church, I fear God's means will be cancer, a car wreck, or an intense season of trial. I believe God when he says the ends will be good, bring glory, and advance the gospel. I'm on board with the ends. I just fear God in the means.

As I consider this truth and acknowledge I am likely not alone with this dark corner of my heart, I offer three things by God's grace I am trying to remember. I hope you will remember them as well.

1) "The light shines in the darkness" (John 1:5). This dark corner is not dark to God. I need to be honest with God and myself. God knows this fear. If anyone knows what it would be like to go through intense difficulty for the glory of God, it is Jesus Christ. He is a man who lost a father, was betrayed by his friends, was hated and challenged at every step, and ultimately was brutally murdered. No part of my heart is hidden from God. It's okay to admit that it's there.

2) "Do not be afraid." This phrase appears roughly thirty-three times in the Scripture. God does not want us to fear. At the same time, he knows he can be scary. He knows life can be strained. He knows faith can be heavy. In reality, God has been much more honest with us about pain than we have been with him. Death may have a sting, but it has no victory. Everything in between is simply the flailing about of a dragon that has already had its head cut off. Christ is risen.

3) "Though He slay me, I will hope in him; yet I will argue my ways to His face" (Job 13:15). While these words were said by Job, a man who experienced the most extreme aspect of my fear, they echo and epitomize the heart of the book of Psalms, the resilience of the prophets, and the steadfastness of the apostles. If Christ Jesus is the cornerstone of a great structure built on the foundation of the apostles and prophets (Ephesians 2:19–22) and I am a brick in this structure, then this confession must be mine as it was of so many who went before. Either way, life will be difficult. Do I want to pretend I can avoid it,

or do I want to embrace the God who allows it and be thankful God has been honest in his word that pain is a part of life? Though it is a part of life, it is not a part of eternity for those in Christ. As a result, I can walk in pain in light of the victory won and the goodness of a God who never leaves or forsakes.

If we read the Scriptures, we know cancer, car wrecks, and catastrophes are just parts of life. We don't have to explain them or try to reconcile them with an idea of a loving God. Love is not always comfortable. I love my wife not only in health but also in sickness. We need a larger perspective and definition of love.

While we may pray for a relief, Christ ultimately provides healing. That may mean healing the heart while the body decays. It may mean rest in the Spirit for one who cannot sleep in the body. It means healing is greater than relieving, and we are healed in Christ.

In reality, this dark corner of my heart is not dark. It's not even a corner. It's the center of a heart struggling between wanting to be the lord of my life and admitting that Jesus Christ is Lord of all. One is fantasy. One is reality. What a wonderful reality that Christ has overcome and has not given us a Spirit of fear (2 Timothy 1:7; Romans 8:15). He is honest. We can be honest with him. In this, we can know the healing already from whatever injury may come. Remember when Jesus said, "I have said these things to you, that in me you may have peace. In the world you will have tribulation. But take heart; I have overcome the world" (John 16:33).

As we finish our time together, we are faced with a reality. You, everyone on this earth, and I need to make a decision about the God we believe in. We must decide whether or not we will willfully and humbly submit to God at all costs as revealed in the Bible. Will we seek God's glory in every avenue, circumstance, and resource? Will we trust, obey, seek to know, and wrestle with the God of the Bible? Or do we prefer a tamer, less confrontational, less risky version that is simply not that God?

Jesus's question to Martha is echoed to us. "I am the resurrection and the life. Whoever believes in me, though he die, yet shall he live, and everyone who lives and believes in me shall never die. Do you believe this?" (John 11:25–26).

If the answer is *yes*, where do we go from here? If the answer is *no*, where do we go from here? My prayer is that you will find life and you will resolve yourself to walk in the truth and reality of Jesus Christ and the gospel. Not every dead man gets raised like Lazarus. But for those in Christ, we have been raised already.

Works Cited

Scripture quotations are from the Holy Bible, English Standard Version (ESV), copyright 2001 by Crossway. Used by permission. All rights reserved.

Endnotes

1   A. W. Tozer, *The Knowledge of the Holy: The Attributes of God, Their Meaning in the Christian Life* (New York: Harper & Row, 1961), 1.

2   Merrill C. Tenney, *John: The Gospel of Belief* (Grand Rapids, MI: Wm. B. Eerdmans Publishing Co., 1976).

3   Ibid.

4   John MacArthur, *The MacArthur New Testament Commentary: John 1-11*, (Moody, 2006).

5   Frederick Dale Bruner. *The Gospel of John: A Commentary.* (Grand Rapids, MI.: W. B. Eerdmans Pub., 2012), 659.

6   Ibid, 660.

7   C.S. Lewis, *Mere Christianity.* (New York: Macmillan, 1958), 190.

8   John MacArthur, *The MacArthur New Testament Commentary: John 1-11*, (Moody, 2006), 450

9   Ibid, 450–451

10 Timothy Keller, *Prayer: Experiencing Awe and Intimacy with God.* (New York: Penguin Group (USA) Incorporated, 2014), 49.

11 Paul Maxwell, "Do You Hate to Wait?" Desiring God. (September 17, 2014. Accessed September 18, 2014), http://www.desiringgod.org/blog/posts/do-you-hate-to-wait.

12 Cole Feix, "The God Who Waits." Address (Sunday Worship Gathering, Stillwater, Oklahoma, June 8, 2014).

13 John Calvin, *John* (Wheaton, IL: Crossway Books, 1994), 274.

14 Joan Powers, and A. A. Milne, *Eeyore's Gloomy Little Instruction Book* (New York: Dutton Books, 1996), 2.

15 Ibid, 4.

16 A. A. Milne, and Ernest H. Shepard, *The House at Pooh Corner* (New York: Dutton, 1961).

17 A.A. Milne, and Ernest H. Shepard, *Winnie-the-Pooh* (New York: Dutton, 1961).

18   Frederick Dale Bruner, *The Gospel of John: A Commentary* (Grand Rapids, MI: W.B. Eerdmans Pub., 2012), 662.

19   John MacArthur, *The MacArthur New Testament Commentary: John 1–11* (Chicago: Moody Press, 2006), 457.

20   William Barclay, *The Gospel of John* (Philadelphia: Westminster Press, 1975), 87.

21   Ibid, 88.

22   Kenneth Silverman, "When the City Was Magical." (*The New York Times*. May 12, 2006), Accessed June 9, 2014.

23   Robin Givhan, "Hubbub in a Bubble." (*Washington Post*. May 6, 2006), Accessed July 10, 2014.

24   R.C. Sproul, *John* (Lake Mary, Fla.: Reformation Trust Pub., 2009), 210.

25   C.S. Lewis, and Pauline Baynes, *The Lion, the Witch, and the Wardrobe* (New York: Harper Trophy), 2000.

26   Merrill C. Tenney, *John, the Gospel of Belief: An Analytic Study of the Text* Pbk. ed. (Grand Rapids, MI: Eerdmans, 1997), 175.

27   John Calvin, *John* (Wheaton, IL: Crossway Books, 1994), 281.

28   Frederick Dale Bruner, *The Gospel of John: A Commentary* (Grand Rapids, MI: W. B. Eerdmans Pub., 2012), 681.

29   Bruce Manning Metzger, *Word Biblical Commentary*. 2nd ed. (Nashville.: Thomas Nelson Publishers, 1999), 194.

30   Frederick Dale Bruner, *The Gospel of John: A Commentary* (Grand Rapids, MI.: W. B. Eerdmans Pub. 2012), 684.

31   Merrill C. Tenney, *John, the Gospel of Belief: An Analytic Study of the Text* Pbk. ed. (Grand Rapids, MI: Eerdmans, 1997), 176.

32   John MacArthur, *The MacArthur New Testament Commentary: John 1–11* (Chicago: Moody Press, 2006), 473.

33   John MacArthur, *The MacArthur New Testament Commentary: John 12–21* (Chicago: Moody Publishers, 2008), 2.

34   R.C. Sproul, *John* (Lake Mary, FL: Reformation Trust Pub., 2009), 217.

35   Frederick Dale Bruner, *The Gospel of John: A Commentary* (Grand Rapids, MI: W. B. Eerdmans Pub., 2012), 691.

36   William Barclay, *The Gospel of John* (Philadelphia: Westminster Press, 1975), 109.

37   John Calvin, *John* (Wheaton, IL: Crossway Books, 1994), 285.

38   C.S. Lewis, *The Complete C. S. Lewis Signature Classics* (New York, NY: HarperOne Publishers, 2002).

Made in the USA
Lexington, KY
01 September 2015